B   2193

Grah

1st PRESBYTERIAN CHURCH
SNOHOMISH WASH.

My Neighbors, the Billy Grahams

Betty Frist

BROADMAN PRESS
Nashville, Tennessee

Dedicated to my husband and my children

© Copyright 1983 • Broadman Press

4272-29

ISBN: 0-8054-7229-0

Dewey Decimal Classification: B

Subject Headings: GRAHAM, BILLY//GRAHAM, RUTH BELL

Library of Congress Catalog Card Number: 83-70368

Printed in the United States of America

Introduction

Over twenty-five years ago, in a partly joking mood, I told Ruth Graham that I might one day write a book about her. The expression on her face prompted me to laugh and say, "You'd like to say to me what Dr. William Lyons Phelps said to a would-be writer who told him, 'Dr. Phelps, when you're gone I plan to write a book about you.' Dr. Phelps answered, 'I know. That's what keeps me going.'" Ruth grinned and said, "You aren't kidding."

So, because she disliked being written about and I disliked writing, I gathered up her neighborly letters and the many notes she'd accused me of "forever scribbling . . . on wretched little scraps of envelopes," and started to burn them.

Something or someone stayed my hand—and from then on I had no real peace until I wrote the book.

I don't claim to have heard a Voice telling me to get on with the book, but for years there were endless impressions coming from many sources—plus some editors who gently prodded me to get something down on paper. In Ruth's book *It's My Turn* she says, "God has never spoken audibly to me, but there's no mistaking when he speaks." Now and then I'd read a verse in the Bible, such as, "In all thy ways acknowledge him and he shall direct thy paths"—and often when I'd pick up my pen, long-forgotten memories came alive.

But because I understood Ruth's dislike of being written about, I found ever-ready excuses to keep from writing.

Finally, after much prayer, the pressures became too great to ignore. Since so much of Ruth's life is devoted to prayer, plus God's answers to those prayers, I outlined in a letter to her the things I felt were God's answers to *my* prayers concerning the book:

1. That I was listening to her instead of to God, who was signaling me from his Word that I was to "Obey God rather than man."

2. That she, herself, could never write an impartial autobiography because the Bible says, "Let another praise thee and not thine own mouth."

3. That her conviction from Scripture that God directs the lives of Christians applied to me as well as to her— and that all the evidence pointed to the fact that God had placed me where he had for one purpose: to write the book.

4. That when I protested to him that as a neighbor and a friend perhaps I didn't have the right to write the book, the impression was "loud and clear" that I didn't have the right to *not* write it. Only a person with such a vantage point would have access to details that would assure that nothing "unimportant" would be left out (which many readers seem to prefer rather than the "important" happenings).

5. That I had more than obeyed her wish to "Wait till the children are grown to write it." (One of the grand-children is almost grown.)

Later, upon going through Ruth's letters and notes from years back, I found two letters from her, giving me permission to write an article about her (which I never did). She'd written, "I trust you. I don't trust me." Then, in spite of her loathing of being written about, she said, "Go ahead . . . I trust you better than I trust myself." Last year she gave me permission to write the book.

But even with her consent, I often felt miserable and kept asking myself, "Why me?" I answered myself with Billy's words when he was asked why he thought God had picked him for his astounding work. He answered, "That's the first question I intend asking him when I get to heaven." I, too.

The feeling persisted that a prominent person rather than a "nobody" should write the book. Then I was reminded of the fact that both Billy and Ruth were "nobodies" in the eyes of the world when God tapped them for service, and that God often picks the most unlikely people and places to carry out his plan. Examples include his choosing "unlearned and ignorant men" for Jesus' apostles rather than highly educated religious leaders (to whom Christ made his most scathing remarks); a stable rather than a palace for Christ's birth; a lowly donkey rather than a spirited prancing steed for his triumphal entry into Jerusalem, and so on. A person can be too big but never too little for the Lord to use.

Since I don't pretend to be any great shakes as a writer, I felt wholly inadequate for the task of writing the book. Then I was reminded of God's words to Moses when he protested God's selection of him to lead the Israelites out of Egypt. "What is that in thine hand?" God asked, concerning the rod carried by Moses. Then God showed him that the rod could be made to accomplish any and every task that God wanted it to accomplish, so I felt that God was saying the same thing to me about the ballpoint pen in my hand.

After completing the book, I recalled an incident from many years back when I sat with Bunny Graham in church when she was a small child. A soloist was singing and Bunny whispered to me, "Is her voice good or bad?" I honestly couldn't tell—and I honestly can't tell whether my book is good or bad. I wish it didn't even have to be called a book, but just a patchwork of odds and ends set down in an informal, diary-type manner. In any event, I've given it to God, mistakes and all, to use or not to use, as he sees fit.

The book has the necessary "repeats" of some incidents published before. (A precedent for this was set in Matthew, Mark, Luke, and John.) I've made the details as accurate as I could remember them, often with the help of notes.

One final concern I had. Many times I prayed about it, telling God that I felt I was too old to bother with all the criticisms that are the necessary and expected part of any book publication. It was then that I received the most vivid and startling impression of the entire time of writing—so vivid that I felt it could have come only from God himself. It came in the form of a question: "Why should you expect *your* book to escape criticism? *Mine* didn't."

Acknowledgments

I would like to thank the following people for their help with this book: Ruth Graham's former secretary, Mrs. Ralph Kyle, and typists Evelyn Goff and Sharon Theriault.

Contents

1. Take the Next Stagecoach Up 9
2. Billy Graham Tried to Sleep Here 24
3. Ruth—Very Much Herself 35
4. Ruth's Parents 51
5. With This Ring 57
6. Ruth as Mother 74
7. The Children's Sayings 81
8. The Trip 84
9. Discipline 91
10. The Faith of the Children 115
11. Potpourri 122
   Cur-few 123
   Cooking and Dining 126
   Race 130
   Excerpts from Letters 132
   The Pool and Cabin 133
   Housekeeping 137
   Education 141
   The Hired Men 145
12. Fun 147

13. Travel 155
14. Thoughtfulness of Parents and Children 163
15. Ruth and Young People 169
16. Friends 177
17. Criticism—Pro and Con 182
18. All This and Heaven Too 195

1

Take the Next Stagecoach Up

If you're planning to look for the Billy Graham property, you may end up wishing you'd stayed home because it's at the end of a scalloped, tortuous mountain road, sometimes called "Coronary Hill." Your car will strain up and up and around like a broken arrow. Chipmunks scurry across the road in front of the car. It's no place for nervous people. A nearby resident says, "I've personally seen two cars with their front ends hanging off into space."

But if you're still determined to find it, keep going until "the air gets thin, your nose begins to bleed and you see buzzards circling" and you'll eventually come on a gate with a sign politely suggesting, "Please turn around here." Of course, the Grahams must maintain their family privacy, of which they have little as a rule.

In 1950 the Grahams bought their approximately two hundred acres on top of the mountain for $4,500. That was in the days before land sold by the square inch and a person owning a grave plot was considered a land baron.

A very old mountaineer told me that when he was

growing up near the Graham property, an acre of land was traded for a musket. (The going rate before that was a handful of beads. Ask any Indian.) However, the old man was insistent that I understand that out of deference to the dove on Noah's Ark, he has never used his musket to shoot one.

Beyond the gate a visitor will pass two little cabins that were on the place when it was bought. One has stodgy, whimsical little fantasy figures on faded blue shutters— painted by Ruth. This cabin has an ell-shaped room, a fireplace, a loft, and a path leading outside. The cabin is completely dehydrated—there was never any running water unless a child ran with a bucket of water from the spring. The other cabin is a little larger, but is fed with water from one of the eighteen springs on the mountain.

Before they moved up the mountain, Billy used this hideaway spot for study and prayer. Someone described such a place as one where a person could go "to let his soul catch up with his body." In Billy's case, it would probably be to let his body catch up with his soul.

One summer Ruth offered one of the cabins to a friend to vacation in, writing in her inimitable way, "Now what's wrong with the little old cabin? Provided the water's turned on, the dead mice fished out of the tub (two in there now), the septic tank doesn't leak all over the place, and no more than six people are squashed in at one time?"

The next description sounded more captivating. "Spring in all its glory is here. Everywhere you look is shimmering chartreuse, bowers of white dogwood, apple blossoms, and violets underfoot. The mountains are brilliant now. This cove is a dream."

About this time, a friend received a letter from Ruth informing her, "We're seriously considering moving up the mountain in another year. For good. Most of the leaves are gone now and you can see—and it's wonderful. Forty bushels of apples are stored in the apple cellar and ten times that many are tempting the bears and yellow jackets as they rot. The spring is just as strong and the little cabin cuter 'n ever—bushels of black walnuts this year and everything tinder dry. The men say there have been bear tracks around the spring." (Ruth goes hunting for a three-hundred-pound bear armed with a camera loaded with film, and Ruth herself is loaded with raw courage.)

Ruth is hooked on log cabins. She wrote, "All I want for my old age is a log cabin with a loft." She doesn't mean the round logs so often seen today but the ancient square-cut logs that were laboriously hewn out by hand with a tool called the broad axe and another one called an adz, which Ruth used to display on the mantel of the fireplace in their guest room.

The house is a layer and a half type and is constructed of this type of log cabin transplants. The cabins had long been on the critical list and were dismantled and brought to the building site.

To Ruth, there's something very special about these old logs which seem to almost pulsate with life. For over a century, they've absorbed and stored the pungent aroma of frying country ham and red eye gravy, freshly baked bread, and bracing hot coffee brewed from newly ground coffee beans. They've plucked from the air the sigh of the old hound dog snoozing by the fire, the low murmurings of lovers, the groans and piercing cries at childbirth, the sounds of muffled sobbing at death, the hoedown beat of the mountain music erupting from the cherished old handmade violins and guitars, and twanging of the musical saws as they formed the backdrop for the wildly gyrating feet of the square dancers. Laughter and prayer also penetrated these walls—all of which adds up to a host of memory flashbacks. History swirls out of the ancient logs and a sense of peace envelops you as you erase from your thoughts the seething chaos of today's living and replace it with the tranquil whisperings of days long gone and the simple joys that were part of those days. At times you feel a deep ache and an intense longing for the return of that shrouded distant past which you well know can live again only in memory.

But not everyone is drawn to log cabins. Ruth's sister, Rosa, who prefers the Chinese decor, would probably consider it a mission of mercy to get Ruth into a more contemporary setting. Asked how Ruth liked *her* house, Rosa said, "She puts up with it."

Several letters Ruth wrote to a friend many years ago about the plans and construction of this house have surfaced to recall those days—

"We have already found one old cabin and had it moved." She mentioned the price as being more than they'd planned to pay, then said, "It was really sweet, though, and they gave me the old spinning wheel that was in it—complete with a set of cards (for wool) and the old sheep shears. We also got the poplar lumber with which it was sealed, the pretty little doors with their handmade hinges, and a sweet little mantel. It was a hundred years old but all the logs except two were sound, and the floor is good enough to use again. We even rescued the rocks from the old chimney." The letter continued, "Now we're trying to locate several more cabins that we can buy. We have six or seven possibilities."

Since Ruth had studied any cabins she could find still standing and pored over any books she could lay her hands on about log cabins, she wanted the chimney rocks laid in the old authentic dry rock fashion. She was willing to have cement used between the rocks for safety and stability, but she didn't want it to show. This was anathema to the twentieth-century rock mason who wanted the cement to upstage the rocks. Finally, in disgust, and with a look of loathing at his work done under Ruth's tutelage, he threw down his tools and walked off the job, saying: "A man can't take no pride in his work up here."

In another letter, Ruth expressed concern that she might have to lock horns with the architect:

"This architect says he has always dreamed of having a client who would turn her plans over to him and then leave for Europe. He's a gem, though—built Oak Ridge for the government and is an authority on Americana. If only he won't be chagrined at my unorthodox ideas and won't feel that they are a reflection on his training and ability."

Ruth knew what she wanted; and when the architect was hesitant about incorporating one of her ideas into his plan, she stuck a pacifier into his mouth by saying, "I'll tell you what, Joe! So you won't get credit for my ideas, when the house is finished, I'll put up a sign in the yard, saying, 'Joe Ware, Architect' and under it, 'Ruth Graham, Counter-Architect.'"

Ruth continued, "I'm not going to be strictly Early American. I don't enjoy being consistent that much and I've seen too many dear little English houses three, four, and five hundred years old." Then she added that she would "probably borrow ideas from them all. But basically it's to be simple, quaint, and homey inside—crude and rustic outside. You'll love it."

One of Ruth's neighbors foolishly bought logs sight-unseen from a neighboring state and had them trucked to her building site. She belatedly asked Ruth to tell her if the logs were good. Ruth turned a professional eye on them and said, "Yes—for firewood." So a search, eventually successful, was begun to find more and better logs.

Some time later, after this neighbor's house was completed, Ruth found that Billy needed more room. So she wrote the neighbor, a summer resident, to ask if she could use some of the leftover logs lying in her yard. The neighbor answered, telling Ruth that she was welcome to use them; but knowing Ruth's penchant for selecting only the finest logs, she added, "Please use the logs lying in our yard and not the ones already cemented into the walls of our house." Ruth wrote back, "Where I removed your logs, I was careful to chink with plenty of your old (antique) quilts, spreads, and rugs."

Things rarely go smoothly in building a house. Ruth is a born artist and, having studied painting, she knows the intricate color shadings. The wrong shade grates on her nerves. The good-natured painter was trying valiantly but unsuccessfully to get the shade she wanted. Finally, one day he had Ruth laughing when he brought her a cartoon showing a painter handing back a cup of coffee to the lady of the house, saying: "This coffee needs to be a shade darker."

Ruth stayed at the job site a good part of the time because there were so many "on the spot" decisions to be made. If a carpenter insisted to Ruth that it was impossible to carry out her idea, her attitude was, "The impossible just takes more time." Ruth confided to a friend, "There's *always* a way to do it."

In any event, if a friend wanted to see Ruth, she knew she had to go to the construction site.

During those days another cartoon was making the rounds. It showed a fancily dressed lady in a flowery hat, lace dress, gloves, and high heels pushing a wheelbarrow full of sloppy, ready-to-pour cement. Beside her, in dungarees, walked the owner of the house being built. The fancy one was saying petulantly, "When you asked me to pour, I thought you meant tea."

Rumors continue rampant about the Grahams's expensive mansion. Today, an antique hand-hewn square-cut log house is considered choice and nonhabit-forming because of rarity. Unless it was put up years ago by a mountain-grown contractor with plenty of cabin know-how, as was the Grahams's, it could be an expensive deal (as is any construction today).

When one politician was asked if he'd been born in a log cabin, he replied reluctantly, "No, but my family moved into one as soon as they could afford it."

During the construction of the house, Ruth found that their bank account went down faster than their house went up, and she announced publicly, "When the bank president calls me, it's not to ask about my health." (Banks are picky about having every cent balance.) Some years ago, I heard this bank president thank Ruth for the publicity her remark had given the bank.

One day the Grahams's mountain contractor told Ruth, "Mizz Graham, you sure know how to squeeze a penny."

Ruth said, "Good, tell that to Bill. He'll be proud of me."

Mr. Sawyer said, "Now you wait just a minute, Mizz Graham. I didn't say whose penny you squeezed."

Some months later, another letter from Ruth arrived in the friend's box.

"I'm writing from the house. It was hectic getting in before Bill arrived. I lost about ten pounds, aged ten years and have a crop of gray hair (Confederate gray, though—writer's note). But anyway, we're in and love it. As Edgar Guest says, 'It takes a heap of livin' to make a house a home,' but this one came as near being homey without living in as any house I've ever seen. And the important thing is that Bill loves it. It's bigger than you or I like, but under the circumstances that was a 'must.' Anyway, it's livable and quiet and we're thrilled over it all.'" Then she'd suddenly burst forth with, "The Lord is so good to us, it makes us ashamed."

The house was necessarily large in order to bed and board the good-sized Graham family, parents and five children plus the endless flow of visitors who have converged on it from all parts of this world—and now, on occasion, in-laws and grandchildren.

Even so, the youngest child spent the first seven years of his life in a handkerchief-sized room which was originally planned to be a closet—but he loved it as well as the whole house and he told Ruth that he wanted to own it one day. She reminded him of the upkeep, insurance, and taxes on such a large place and asked him if he thought he could afford it. He said, "Sure." Then he cut his eyes around at her and added, "As long as my wife works."

Of course, with all the children married, the house now has a baggy fit except for the reunions when the entire family connection comes home—which is as often as they can arrange it. Ruth has had the heating system redesigned with thermopane windows upstairs separated by doors from downstairs.

Rumors also continue unabated about the so-called expensive furniture in the Graham home.

In the main, it's furnished with simple mountain pieces that Ruth picked up here and there through the mountains. A friend laughs and says that some of the people who sold her the furniture felt they should have paid her rather than charged her to take it off their hands.

At first, Billy felt the same way. He found it difficult to welcome with open arms some of Ruth's "as is" choices. One day in a friend's home, he pointed to a sorry-looking antique that was in line for refinishing and said, "That's the kind that Ruth likes."

Because of his attitude, whenever Ruth would buy an antique, she'd put it in her car trunk and say jokingly to a friend (whose husband felt the same way Billy did): "If Billy sees it first, it's yours. If your husband sees it first, it's mine."

Well aware of the difference of opinion between them, a friend produced a cartoon which was guaranteed to make both of them laugh. It pictured a crowd gathered at an antique auction. The auctioneer was holding up an antique and saying, "Sold to the woman with her husband's hand over her mouth."

But even though Ruth bought comfortable overstuffed furniture for the living room, she said that Billy would invariably head for the frail antique rocker near the fireplace. She'd wait for the crash as he lowered his big frame into it.

Ruth's mother also took a dim view of some of Ruth's purchases. After seeing her pay cash on the barrelhead for several battered pieces that needed intensive care, she pointed to an old beat-up piece in the dusty antique shop and said, "Ruth, why don't you buy that? It's rotten too."

There were other discouragements. The Grahams's little daughter, GiGi, who was a crack Bible student, told Ruth worriedly, "Mother, you aren't going to be happy in heaven with your antiques because the Bible says, "Old things are passed away and behold, all things are become new."

Some years after the furnishing of the house had been in the news, there was a piece of furniture owned by a friend that Ruth particularly liked and wanted to buy. Finally, after much pro and con chatter between them, the friend wrote Ruth telling her that she believed (as does Billy) that the Lord's return wasn't too many years away and that she couldn't care less about keeping the piece—offering it to Ruth. Ruth fired off a letter to her. "You're sneaky. Your letter was like offering a chocolate soda to an overweight person. I'm looking for the Lord to come too, yet you want me to get caught with a house full of furniture while you busily 'lay up treasure in heaven.'"

When Muhammed Ali visited the Graham home, he was expecting a mansion. But he appreciated greatly the hominess of the Graham property.

A friend, looking at a magazine picture of Billy and Ruth seated before an antique cupboard in their living room, laughed and said, "I know how much that piece cost because I gave it to them. I paid fifteen dollars for it. I also gave them another one of their living room pieces, and I paid under twenty-five dollars for it." Then she added, grinning, "Of course, that was before Jesse James was working the cash register."

One of Ruth's letters, written a while after they had moved into the house, tells a friend:

"I haven't bought anything since you left except the old cupboard which the people never got around to collecting. Oh, yes—I did buy seven old patchwork quilts for four dollars each. They aren't exactly museum pieces but they've got atmosphere."

After the furniture went through a renovating process and was restored to its natural beauty, Billy thought it was beautiful. One day he called one of Ruth's friends and asked her to go to a nearby antique show to pick out a piece for him to give Ruth on their anniversary. The friend jokingly asked, "How much do you want me to pay for it?—five hundred dollars?" There was a dead silence at the other end of the line and when Billy recovered his voice he said, "The silence you heard was me passing out." (The friend said he never called her again to shop for him.)

Sometime later another hurried letter recorded: "We've done a little remodeling. In February I went to Hawaii with Bill, as you know, and came home and pitched into a lightening and brightening campaign. Old brown hall is painted white—so is upstairs hall. So is dining room (instead of cream). Bill's study is remodeled to give him a little more light and privacy. The red carpet is relaid in hall going from our bedroom, up the stairs and down the upstairs hall. Bill's study is bright gold. Cut another window and replaced the three casements behind the desk with a long picture window. The TV room is getting fixed into a bedroom for him (due to a cough Ruth developed that kept both of them awake all night). Same gold carpeting with ceiling to match and palest yellow walls. It's really lovely—ever so much lighter, less formal and lovelier. More relaxing. Also having sofa and chair in the living room slipcovered."

The letter continued, "But spring is just around the corner and we'll be turning all our attention outdoors."

I've known Ruth to make lamps out of tin cans or anything she could find to work with, in order to save money. The result was usually "electrifying" and sometimes "stunning." Billy panned them because he was afraid they'd blow out all the transformers in the area.

For many years the Grahams's bed springs and mattress rested on cement blocks as an economy measure.

Twice in the years I've known Ruth, I've seen her sitting in the middle of the old living room rug surrounded by bottles of dye and brushes, trying to perk up the faded leaves and flowers for a few more gasps. They still have the rug.

In the days when Ruth was shopping for furniture for the house, she wrote a friend about another of her friends who had gone "junking" with her and said, "She's no more help than you are, encouraging me to buy things I can't afford."

On one occasion a friend *did* pressure Ruth into buying a piece that Ruth felt cost more than she should have paid, though it was very reasonably priced. Because it kept pricking her conscience, she wasted no time getting rid of it.

Though Billy and Ruth aren't holding out a tin cup, due to property inheritance, income from books and other journalistic recognition, as well as good investments and a reasonable salary, they haven't forgotten the days when finding a dime in the pocket of last winter's jacket was cause for rejoicing.

Most of the time the house inside and out is a welter of flowers—a veritable flower basket. Large geraniums were Ruth's specialty, but since the wilderness is closing in on them, she has replaced geraniums with begonias and impatiens. Her flower boxes are something to behold. The variegated flowers in them strut in their flamboyantly colored plumage in a blaze of glory against the tannish gray log walls.

Once in the Graham home, a fortunate guest is soon deeply absorbed in Ruth's own brand of hospitality, which is so enticing that a guest is often tempted to extend his visit—and often has done so. One guest suggested that Ruth hook into the guest room rug the reminder, "You are leaving Monday, aren't you?"

If a person is exhausted from a long, tiring trip, he'll soon find himself fed and bedded down in an outsized copy of an Early American bed which Ruth had custom made by a local carpenter for twenty-five dollars. Either you come out of it by steps or parachute down. It has the spacious feeling of a football field with plumped-up pillows in abundance. Its linens are snowy white sheets and coverlids from Scotland, or wherever, because there are few places Ruth hasn't gone. One spread is handmade of the early type punchwork design in a grape pattern, fringed. Under the bed is an antique trundle bed with its old quilt coverings.

In addition to the antique pieces in the room, there is an interesting piece with intricate inlaid work made by Ruth's grandfather, who was tops in his field. There's also a fireplace in the room; and when one of the sons was six or seven he'd often come in and start a cheerful fire for the guest—then make coffee from beans ground in an antique grinder, which had the harmonious sound of stripped gears when it was being turned.

Over the large drive-in type fireplace in the living room is a massive beam which was once the diving board at Lake Susan in Montreat where they live. Carved in its face are the never-to-be forgotten words from the hymn by Martin Luther which shout to the world, "A mighty fortress is our God." In the center of the mantel is an antique blue and white platter which Ruth picked up in Scotland. It arrived in many pieces and Ruth, undaunted, glued it together and gave it the place of honor on the mantel. She's equally good at patching up broken lives.

Sometimes, if the down draft of the fireplace isn't just right, it smokes like a diesel engine until it gets under way; but that's rare. In bygone years the family would occasionally gather there to cook steaks, but more often they were cooked on the porch or in the yard where the view is spectacular.

Every room in the house has Ruth's unique imprint and is breathtakingly charming. Any one of the rooms would be perfectly at home gracing the cover of the slick decorator magazines, and it isn't necessary that a person have the key to Fort Knox to open the door to these rooms. Ruth has proved that a room can have a mouth-watering effect without being overly expensive.

As a "do it yourself" decorator, Ruth refuses to be poured into a mold. She does exactly what she wants to do. Sometimes she displays elegant silver in an old pine cupboard. Sometimes the curtains against the living room log walls are Early American, yellow and white checked gingham, but at times she startles your eye by putting sheer embroidered curtains against the rough walls. If she finds a color she likes in a satin material, she'll turn it wrong side out and use the dull backside for slip covers or pillows.

Ruth is fiercely independent about many things; and though many people are "leaders with no followers," Ruth is a natural-born leader—yet also one of the most dedicated followers of Christ that you'll ever meet.

After observing Billy and Ruth for many years, sometimes at close hand, sometimes afar off through letters, magazines, books, and crusade reports, I feel that the following story is apropos of their feelings and attitudes about their material possessions:

There was a saintly black woman who seemed to draw trouble like a magnet, but none of the adversity shook her faith in God. She continued to face life cheerfully and serenely. Then came the day when her house and all her possessions went up in smoke. Even that catastrophe failed to ruffle her confidence in God. When an incredulous friend asked her how she could still trust God in the face of what he had let happen to her, she answered reverently and with a glow as from another world on her face: "Well, I'll tell you, honey. Long ago, I gave the Lord everything I owned. And all I can say is, he's just gone and burned up his own stuff." She was expressing in a vivid, homey way the attitude that all Christians should have about the "things" that often clutter their lives.

Although the Graham home is as comfortable and photogenic a place as one would ever hope to see, Billy and Ruth look on it as temporary housing—a place to live until the Lord calls them to the eternal home that he's preparing for them in heaven.

He's promised them as well as all who trust in him alone for salvation, "In my Father's house are many mansions: If it were not so, I would have told you. I go to prepare a place for you. And if I go . . . I will come again, and receive you unto myself; that where I am, there ye may be also" (John 14:2-3).

Billy and Ruth are ready to leave at a moment's notice.

2

Billy Graham
Tried to Sleep Here

ᒪᒪ

A loud scream bit into the Sunday calm and with it was heard the screeching of brakes. Someone shouted, "There he is," and the stampede was on. A sightseer had spotted a bewildered Billy Graham before he could take cover in his North Carolina home.

That was many years ago.

Among some old papers of that period, I picked up a yellowed dog-eared New York City paper picturing Ruth and their three little girls meeting Billy as he arrived from Europe on the *Queen Mary* after his spectacularly successful crusades there. The account records that he spoke to 2,047,333 people and employed 80 secretaries to answer the 10,000 letters a week.

The account continues, "Among the other 1,689 passengers on the *Queen Mary* were actors Jimmy Stewart and Spencer Tracy but it was the blond, fast-talking, energetic preacher who attracted most attention."

This was only a hint of things to come. After that, Billy's popularity, prestige, and impact on the world catapulted to such staggering heights that any expression found in any language seemed too frail to carry the load of this phenomenon, sometimes even spoken of as the Billy Graham Phenomenon.

Ruth was suddenly thrust into the middle of all this acclaim and, being a naturally private person, was floored by it all. From the first flush of fame, she experienced an acute distaste for the limelight. She hated the feeling that she was roped off for viewing. She's often said, with a trace of hopelessness, "All I want is anonymity and oblivion."

When an acquaintance assured her, grinning, "You'll get used to the publicity," Ruth said vehemently, "I'll *never* get used to it." And she hasn't, but she's willing to go through the misery of being written about in order to faithfully witness to Christ in a day when so many are "hostile witnesses."

A friend, laughing, said, "I don't think fame would be so bad," and Ruth replied, "You just wait till I have a sign painted, 'To the Billy Grahams,' and point it down the road to your house!"

Day in and day out cameras clicked and whirred, gobbling up everything in sight. Their yard became as private as a state park with souvenir hunters chipping off pieces of the gate. Buses let out passengers and they took over the yard, even peering in the windows at the family. It looked like Dawson City at the height of the Gold Rush.

On one occasion when Ruth was pregnant, she hurried into the bedroom to escape being photographed, only to find a camera pointed at her through the window. A friend, knowing her aversion to cameras, said, exaggerating a little, "Ruth would just as soon have a cannon as a camera pointed at her."

On arriving home from the hospital with a new baby in her arms, Ruth was almost made a candidate for the hospital emergency room when Billy told her he'd meant to surprise her by having all the foliage around the house cut down. The foliage was the one thing she counted on for privacy.

Billy sometimes crawled on the floor between windows to escape detection.

In those early days of fame, the Baptists were the worst offenders because Billy is a Baptist and the Baptist conference center is just down the road from their home. However, when they understood the situation, they tried to cooperate. (Many people don't understand why Billy is a Baptist and Ruth remains a Presbyterian, but one of the little Graham girls explained it satisfactorily to me. She said, "Men are Baptists and women are Presbyterians.")

During the days of the Baptist influx, the Grahams owned a pet dog named Belshazzar. You had to see him to believe him. He looked like a cross between a polar bear and a pony, and his aim in life was to get everybody in the obituary column. Ruth defended him by saying in jest, "He can't bite you. He's lost all his teeth." They probably came out in somebody's leg.

I once told Ruth, "That dog would bite anybody!" Ruth said, with mock sorrow, "No, he won't bite a Baptist."

I asked, "May I tell what you just said if I make it clear that you were joking?"

"Why say I was joking?" she countered. But for those whose sense of humor might be in eclipse, she *was* joking, and later mused, "I wish it were possible for a dog to be converted."

When Ruth and Billy found that one of the tiny girls, a show-stealer, was posing for pictures at the gate and collecting fees on the side, they made hurried plans to move up the mountain where they now live in a spot secluded and remote enough to harbor those bear tracks already mentioned.

During those hectic days, Ruth was asked by a reporter how the children were being affected by their daddy's fame. Her matter-of-fact reply: "They think all daddies are famous."

Every one of the children has kept a levelheaded attitude toward fame through all the years of starring in everything from "Brownie stills" to professional movie shots.

A friend recalls that she was walking with the three little Graham girls when a carload of sightseers stopped to ask directions to the Graham home. The children stared trancelike ahead, never giving an inkling as to who they were. The woman who had them in tow commented, "If the car occupants had taken time to look, they would have seen that one of the little girls was almost a stencil of Billy." (At that time, the Montreat gate boys banded together to try to protect Billy. If someone coming through the gate asked where Billy Graham lived, they'd either ask, "Who's he?" or give directions so complicated and unreliable that, if followed, they might land the inquirers at the Asheville jail.)

A visitor in the home recalls that one morning the front page of the paper showed Billy pictured with the current president. She said to one of the children, "Do you want to see a picture of your daddy with the president?" The child gave it a quick onceover and asked indifferently, "Is that supposed to be important?" and went back to her play.

One day a teenage boy walked into the airport that feeds their home area. He had on ratty-looking, faded clothes, and his hair looked like it had been combed with an eggbeater. A man was heard to exclaim, "That boy looks enough like Billy Graham to be his son." It was, and he always seemed unimpressed by the fame surrounding him.

The Graham children had their own way of dealing with sightseers. They were as alert as fox terriers; and whenever they heard the sound of a car engine slowing down, the "lookout" would shriek, "Peoples is comin'." They'd all dive for cover behind tree trunks, bushes, garbage cans, or anything that afforded temporary protection. One man who came into the yard looked at the children and said, "I feel like I'm on holy ground." He wasn't disillusioned by being told that the little Grahams had just been trying to take each other apart in a fight to the finish.

One little one who looked like a delicate figurine once asked, "Can't we please have a little privacy," but spoke only to herself as she was too shy at that time to say it to a visitor.

Ruth was greatly embarrassed the day the baby turned the hose on a hapless visitor who came into the yard uninvited. She always pleaded with the children to be kind to the visitors—telling them that they were friends, not enemies. But it was increasingly hard for little children to be wrenched from their play to be polite to complete strangers—especially when crawfish were getting away in the stream.

Even after they moved up the mountain, their comparatively inaccessible home remained under siege, the road to it sometimes resembling the Pennsylvania Turnpike. Consequently, courteous signs along the road announced,

"Please turn around here," "Private, please!" and "Dangerous dogs."

Ruth, whose raffish sense of humor surfaces in spite of herself, posted a sign near the home, "Trespassers will be eaten." But before a visitor reached that sign, there was another one on which the painter had misspelled a word. Ruth's father kept suggesting that she have it corrected. Finally Ruth asked, "Why? If they get that far up they can't read anyway."

One day an interested friend asked Ruth where the children were. She answered, tongue in cheek, "Probably trying to push each other off the cliff at the back of the house." When the friend mentioned that the cliff was a dangerous place, Ruth became very serious and her mouth tensed as she asked gravely, "Is the cliff really more dangerous than the visitors who try to make the children feel important?"

Then as she and the friend started down the mountain in the car, she recovered her sense of humor enough to call back to the children, "Watch out for bears and visitors."

On another occasion a man knocked at the Graham door and asked to see Billy. When told he was working on a radio program and couldn't be disturbed, he left with tears in his eyes. When Billy heard about it he ran down the mountain until he caught up with him, giving him the spiritual help he sought and the financial help he needed.

On another occasion, a stranger suddenly appeared uninvited in Billy's bedroom. Billy was startled and asked him what he wanted. When the interloper gave no reply, Billy took him by the arm to lead him out. The man made a movement that made Billy think he was reaching for a gun. Knowing he had the responsibility of defending his turf—mainly Ruth and the children—Billy used a wrestling grip he had learned in college on the man, knocking him to the floor. Then he helped him up, dusted him off, and took him out to a waiting car, where the father told Billy his son was a mental patient.

Another man appeared at the church Billy attends when he's home. He was carrying a suitcase which he said contained a bomb. Even though it turned out to be a Bible, the security guard came in and sat in the pew with him, just behind Billy and Ruth. The stranger had failed to see them come in. Billy was told that the man wanted to see him, and it was suggested that he slip out of the church by the back door. Billy refused, insisting that he wanted to talk with the man. However, the man, obviously mentally disturbed, must have felt trapped. He suddenly leaped up and hurried out of the church, where he was taken into protective custody until his relatives in another state could come for him.

Not all of the visitors were alcoholic or mental patients—some were just determined. One such appeared at the door, determined to see Billy. Ruth was just as determined he shouldn't. He quickly knocked into a cocked hat all the reasons Ruth gave as to why Billy couldn't be disturbed. Finally, with bulldog tenacity and a clenched fist attitude, he told Ruth, "I would still like to see him for a few minutes!" Ruth, who has so little time with Billy even when he's home, said wistfully, "So would I."

When Billy wondered at the number of people who continued to show up, Ruth laid part of the blame at his door. She said that in the early days of his radio programs and crusades, Billy would tell his listeners to stop by and see them if they were ever in Montreat. Smiling, she said, "They did."

Ruth also good-naturedly blames Billy at times for her own lack of privacy. Billy is proud of her and wants people to know her. Several times in crusades he's gone to the mike and asked her to come to the platform. Getting no response, he'd try again. Ruth would hunch lower in her seat. When the vast audience would crane its collective neck looking for her, Ruth would assume a look as inscrutable as a barbershop Indian and crane hers along with theirs. Finally, Billy would give her up as a "missing person" and she'd settle down to be just another person among thousands.

She hates publicity because, as she says, "I either have to 'live up to it' or 'live it down.'" Consequently, she has to be almost flogged into print. Also, she feels that Christian should be shown "up" rather than "off." The result is that she'd rather be under the platform than on it.

How do Ruth's friends feel about the ongoing fame? Because Ruth is out of circulation when Billy comes home, her friends call him "The Plague."

One of Ruth's schoolfriends wrote, "I'd like to write Ruth but I hate to bother her while she's being Mrs. Billy Graham." When Ruth heard about it, she sat down and wrote her.

Even close friends have been guilty of adding to the stress. One friend told Ruth that it would mean so much to her if she could bring a few of her relatives to see their house. Ruth later said to another friend, her voice faintly strained, "But all of my friends have relatives."

Some years ago, Ruth sent a check to one of her young friends who was working with the poor in India. He wrote his mother asking her to tell Ruth that he couldn't get it cashed since nobody knew her there. His mother said she was afraid to tell Ruth for fear she'd rush out and buy a one-way ticket to India in order to get relief from the goldfish-bowl type of life she's forced to live here.

Even on the golf course Billy is ringed by prying eyes. One story is told of a golfer who heard that Billy was to be on that particular golf course at a certain time. He called his wife in a nearby state to tell her to take a plane to a nearby airport to make it to the golf course in time to see Billy pass.

But not everybody around golf courses gives him that kind of obeisance. It's been reported that one little old lady, living on one of the golf courses he sometimes plays on, couldn't care less about his fame. She flails him with her tongue just like she does anybody else when his ball strays into her yard. (This attitude is more refreshing to Billy than the attitude, "Make way for the king," which he often encounters.)

Almost everywhere Billy goes he's immediately recognized. Some time ago, he and the family were returning from a family reunion in Charlotte. He had to stop the car at Old Fort to have chains put on the tires so he could make it up the heavily iced mountain to their home a few miles away. They stopped at a gas station across the street from a church where services were being conducted. The enterprising minister in the pulpit caught a glimpse of Billy through the church window and rushed out of the church, collared him, and brought him inside for a short talk to the surprised and grateful congregation.

Now and then Billy's fame fails to bring the expected results. On one occasion when Billy was ill, a bed was made for him in the backseat of his car. T. W. Wilson, who accompanied him as staffer, buffer, and friend, was driving him through the night to get him home and in bed.

In order to stay awake, T. W. drove into an all-night roadside stand parking lot and, intent on not waking Billy, eased himself out of the car and went in to get a cup of coffee which he hurriedly gulped. When he came out, he slipped noiselessly under the steering wheel and headed down the homestretch toward Montreat, a state away.

In the meantime, Billy had waked up and gone to the rest room. When he came out the car and his coat were gone. Cold, ill, and feverish, he went into the diner, identified himself, told his story, and offered payment to anyone who would drive him home. The customers apparently thought he was a look-alike, pulling their legs, and there were no takers. So Billy had to hire a car and drive himself home, somehow eluding the police who had been alerted immediately after T. W. drove into a lighted gas station and looked around in horror at the empty backseat. Paul Harvey, recounting the event, remarked that Billy would get over it but that T. W. never would.

For those who have tried and failed to get the Grahams by phone (which one of the little children called the "I'll get it!"), they can shrug off some of their frustration by remembering Billy's experience.

As I remember it, when he was in Europe, he tried to call Ruth. Because their phone number is unlisted and also frequently changed, Billy had forgotten his latest number, which the operator refused to give him. Trying to clarify the situation, he told the operator that it was Billy Graham, himself, on the line. She said, "I know it's you, Dr. Graham, because I listen to you on the radio and recognize your voice, but I still can't give you your number."

Billy chuckled, thanked her for refusing to be a party

to an infraction of the rules, then called his father-in-law who lived near them and got the number.

With the overwhelming pressures of the brutally packed days of speaking engagements and diversified responsibilities, Billy has said publicly several times that he'd be so happy if the Lord would call him home. But even with the glories of heaven beckoning, he's been denied the luxury of dying.

Paul looked forward to the same thing, exulting, "Absent from the body, . . . present with the Lord" (2 Cor. 5:8).

3
Ruth—Very Much Herself

Ruth is strictly herself, which seems to suit everyone who knows her. Though she buys many of her clothes at more expensive stores, she keeps an eagle eye on the reduced racks and gets as much mileage as possible out of her carefully selected wardrobe. For many years there's been a brisk little poem stuck in the mirror in her dressing room ending with the sentiment, "Make the old one do."

Thrifty habits of childhood still have remote control over her. She speaks with joy of the days in China where her mother, a missionary nurse, dressed her attractively out of the mission barrel, hoping she wouldn't look like the "pickins'" from it. Her sewing machine went full speed ahead, putting Dior-type touches on someone's castoff clothing.

Ruth remembers that when she entered Wheaton College, she arrived with one good homemade dress—and a meager school wardrobe. Accessories were a homemade scarf and a string of ten-cent-store pearls.

She inherited her mother's talent for sewing. In the

days before her time was severely rationed with its "Light, Camera, Action" existence, she made her own clothes, even to faultlessly tailored suits. But after attending a posh celebration in Europe, she wrote a friend, "All those elegant people and me in a homemade dress with zipper trouble."

Ruth is the tailored type and confesses that the flowered hat she wore as speaker at the women's section of the President's Prayer Breakfast was a concession to Billy, who now and then likes to see her in more frilly attire.

Ruth's housemother at college recalled that Ruth, in addition to being very attractive, had excellent taste in clothes.

In her position as the wife of a world-famous evangelist, Ruth is adamant in feeling that she shouldn't flaunt expensive clothes and jewelry. However, she admits to liking lovely jewelry and says that if she were the wife of a Texas millionaire, she might succumb to the temptation to wear it.

When she was given a thousand-dollar gift certificate from Neiman-Marcus, she bought a gold bracelet, then gave it to a son to auction off for charity.

Johnny Cash and his wife, June, gave her a hooded mink coat which, with their permission, was given as a donation to charity. A wealthy friend bought it and returned it to Ruth as a birthday gift, stipulating that Ruth keep it this time. Not too long ago, Billy gave away the fact that he and Ruth give away five hundred thousand dollars each year and added that they were also planning to give up some things that they may have held on to more tightly than they should have.

Ruth habitually bought the family's shoes at stores that sold quality brand shoes at greatly reduced prices. One day when the clerk asked her what size she wore, she said, grinning, with her eyes crinkling at the edges like seersucker, "Any size that's on sale." (Recently two of the Graham daughters were home; and, though neither of them carries a flat wallet, they were headed for the same shoe stores. The passing years have failed to wean them away from their favorite shopping places.)

As to makeup, Ruth wears only enough to keep her from looking wan, and Billy encourages her in it. One day an overly pious woman approached him and said, rather smugly, "Dr. Graham, I don't wear makeup of any kind." Billy remarked, with kindly concern, "You should. You need it."

In reference to her own makeup, Ruth, with one of her disarming grins, told a large gathering of women about a man who, totally disapproving of any makeup and in sympathy for Billy, said, "Billy has enough troubles without having a bad woman for a wife."

Even as a child, Ruth showed indelible signs of being the woman she is today. A retired missionary who lived in the same compound with Ruth's family when she was a child, reminiscing, said, "The missionaries used to ask each other, 'Well, what has Ruth done or said this time?'"

Ruth has a notorious inability to be insipid in anything she says or does. When a reporter asked her if Billy ever entertained doubts, she said, "He has them; he doesn't entertain them."

A friend was trying to pick Ruth's brain for a title to an article she was writing on teenagers. In the course of the conversation, she said to Ruth, "I'm for teens," and Ruth said, "Then call it Pro-teens."

One young friend of Ruth's told his mother, "I love Ruth. She's so homely." Though his description might not pass a dictionary test, his mother knew what he meant and heartily agreed. Ruth is homey, down to earth—a relaxing over-the-back-fence type of person.

I've never known her to go to a beauty parlor, though there may have been emergencies when she has. She's always shampooed and set her own hair. Before the advent of the hair dryer, she dried hers in the oven. When this was mentioned to her some time ago, she said, "I hate to admit it, but I still do."

One day Ruth walked through their living room exuding a heady fragrance. When a guest in the room asked the name of her perfume, she said, "Bathroom Spray," and continued to the kitchen.

Ruth is also the perfect example of the nonfrenzy. On one occasion an agitated teacher sent her a note telling her that her first grader sometimes came to school with wrinkled clothes, like he'd slept in them. Ruth penciled on the note, "They are, and he has," and sent it back to her. He'd gone through a time of being afraid he'd be late to school, so he'd take his bath, then put on clean clothes and sleep in them. Ruth refused to make a killer whale out of a sardine.

One night at dinner in their home, a guest with a bald spot and a quizzical expression kept feeling his head. Then he said, "Ruth, it feels like sawdust is falling on my head." Ruth, unperturbed, said, "It is" without missing a beat in the conversation. She doesn't come unglued over the wood borers who have taken up residence in the massive beams overhead. She said facetiously that she could hear them chewing but also insisted that a shot of insect spray could put them out of commission until the next time. When a guest glances up, he's startled to see a tiny gremlin with an Afro hairdo staring out at him from one of the knotholes in the beam—another evidence of Ruth's droll sense of humor.

One evening Ruth had just finished shampooing her hair and rolling it on curlers when there was a knock at the door. On answering it, she found a VIP and his wife who had arrived for dinner at Billy's invitation—and he'd forgotten to tell her. Ruth didn't make a federal case out of it because emergencies are routine with the Grahams.

Ruth has definite convictions and also the courage to stand behind them, though she does it with rare good humor. When asked if she believed in Women's Lib, she said with her eyes twinkling, "Yes, I believe that women should be liberated from all outside work so they can stay home and take care of their children."

It's been said that a person becomes mature when he can laugh at himself. Ruth can.

Billy has been an almost nonstop global traveler during much of their married life. Because of that, he's spoken publicly many times to say that Ruth has had the responsibility of rearing the children, managing the house, and making the decisions that are often made by the man in the home. When he was given the title Father of the Year, he said it should have gone to Ruth.

Ruth remains humble and unassuming. After reading a newspaper account about Ruth and certain of her friends whose names were often in print, a friend jokingly wrote her about hobnobbing with important people. Back came a letter saying, "It doesn't pay to feel important. The only time I ever walked across a stage feeling important, I found out later that my slip was showing. The Lord has a way of cutting us down to size, too. But I hope not to give him another opportunity."

One day I heard a singer belting out, "I won't go huntin' with you, Jake, but I'll go chasin' women." Years ago Stewart Hamblin of West Coast fame (now famous for writing songs like "This Old House" and "It Is No Secret What God Can Do") was led to Christ by Billy and Ruth when he called them in their hotel room in the early morning hours. He was in such a spiritually distraught condition that Billy and Ruth didn't take time to dress but received him in their bathrobes.

After his conversion he was so upset over the record about chasing women that he bought up as many as he could find and smashed them to smithereens. Ruth said she hid one of them in order to show the transforming power of Christ in a person's life.

One day a boy in his early teens, accompanied by his mother, had gone to the home of Ruth's parents to watch Billy's televised crusade from Madison Square Garden. Billy preached a masterful sermon on the biblical teaching that the man should be the head of the house, supporting it with Scripture. As they left the house after the telecast was over, the teenager said to his mother, "That was a great sermon and I know two people who needed it, you and Ruth Graham."

When Ruth heard about it, she laughed and said, "Don't tell Bill."

Ruth seems entirely without fear in a day when a howling panic stalks the earth, when the faces of timid souls are pewter colored with terror, and when even the more stalwart among us are handcuffed to a nameless fear.

Ruth's father, in speaking of Ruth's temporary stay on top of the mountain by herself, said, "She seems to like staying up there alone—doesn't know what fear really is." (Ruth gives much of the credit for her lack of fear to her parents who never showed fear—and also to promises made by God in his Word.)

For many years there's been an automatic machine in Billy's room which spews out the latest news, some items good but many very frightening. For those who trust God, he counteracts the frightening ones. His Word says: "He shall not be afraid of evil tidings: his heart is fixed, trusting in the Lord" (Ps. 112:7). Those who have Ruth's courage are able to say, in the words of the Bible: "I will trust, and not be afraid" (Isa. 12:2). Those with trembling, fearful hearts can have steel put into their backbones by relying on the words of the psalmist, who said confidently, "What time I am afraid, I will trust in thee" (Ps. 56:3).

Because of the steadily spiraling crime rate, Ruth and a friend were discussing the number of ominous and sinister-sounding news items. Ruth suddenly burst forth, her voice vibrant, "But isn't it an exciting time to be alive?"

Ruth's mother told me of one incident that occurred when Ruth was a tiny child in China. Bandits were approaching the missionary compound where they lived, and the shooting was getting closer and closer and louder and louder. Mrs. Bell hurried toward Ruth's room, intent on quelling her fears, and called out, "Ruth, there's nothing to be afraid of." She heard Ruth answer cheerily, "Who's afraid?"

This attitude has been typical of her throughout her life. When she was a little older, she was so devoted to Christ that her all-consuming desire was to be a martyr for him. Every day she'd pray fervently and audibly that God would allow the bandits to capture and behead her.

Her sister, Rosa, hearing her, would pray in concern (and probably a little exasperation): "Lord, don't listen to her."

At the Billy Graham Day in Charlotte, Billy's hometown, President Nixon was the key speaker. He had high praise for both Billy's mother and Ruth, saying that the women in the Graham family were the "stronger." Many would agree. Billy says of his mother that she picked beans nearly all day the day he was born and that the next day she was out picking beans again.

Many will remember the time when it was falsely rumored that Billy himself might be available for the office of president. Switchboards in the area lit up to handle the calls, and at the local post office it wasn't just "business as usual."

One of Ruth's friends says she foolishly joined in the fringes of the clamor for Billy to throw his hat in the ring and wrote Ruth to that effect.

She got a knee-jerk reaction from Ruth that showed how important Ruth considered Billy's work.

The letter read, "If I weren't absolutely convinced of your sanity, I'd be tempted to think your European tour had affected your mind. Bless you. Bill in the pulpit, I am one hundred percent for. Bill in the White House (or campaigning for it) leaves me cold. Not up his alley. Of course I love anyone who believes in my Bill. And I deeply appreciate your vote of confidence, as it were. But I feel quite deeply that his present job is more important. He is first and foremost a preacher, not an administrator. It isn't a question of ability, but of calling."

Then she added, "The young one is cute as pie. We're happily preparing for Christmas, minus Bill. But this trip to Korea is such a wonderful opportunity." (He spent Christmas with the troops there.)

Ruth is a mixture of flint and thistledown. She's fragile looking, almost wraithlike in appearance, but she's made of the heavy-duty material that characterized the tough saddlebag frontier type of pioneer woman. She probably would have won hands down the title, "Woman of the Year 1776."

A friend says, "She's a human dynamo. I've seen her haul rocks in a jeep, tie heavy chains around a tree stump, connect it to the jeep, and jerk it out of the ground."

A letter from Ruth confirmed it. "Well, I'll be seeing you in just a few weeks and we'll drink gallons of coffee and then I'll probably have to pull the rest of the stumps out of your yard and we'll have another wonderful summer." (This was before coffee was accused of being an all-out culprit.)

But Ruth is equally at home when she's exquisitely and daintily gowned and presiding over a perfectly appointed tea table.

Franklin says of her, "My mother is feisty. She's also sweet."

Ruth's mother used to say of her as a child, "She's such a tenderhearted little thing," and she still is a wonderfully tenderhearted person. But if the occasion demands, she can be the unquestioned leader of the mule train. Referring to a legal case from years back that was settled in her favor, she said, her voice stiffening, "If the judge had fined me, I'd have gone to jail before I'd paid it."

In the next breath, she'd have her friends doubled up with laughter as she'd tell how, in her teenage years, she'd make prospective dates disappear like licked cotton candy when she'd announce primly, "I don't smoke, drink, or pet." But those "in the know" concerning those dating years hint that she had to sweep would-be suitors off her doorstep.

Ruth, being very attractive, has drawn her share of wolves. Many times during the London Crusade, she'd walk incognito through the crowds in the park, hoping to pick up remarks about the crusade. One day a wolf tried to pick *her* up. She tried to walk away from him but he followed, so she decided to try to see what made him tick, help him, and invite him to the crusade.

He quickly noted her accent and asked where she was from. She told him, "The United States." He asked, "You aren't by any chance with the crusade, are you?" Ruth answered, "Yes." He was looking a little less ardent but didn't seem to know how to put a period to the conversation. He was tailgating trouble when he asked, "Are you married?" Ruth again replied, "Yes."

"Not to one of the team members," he asked hopefully, but his face was clearly showing distress signals. Ruth again said, "Yes" and was thoroughly enjoying the look of incredulity gathering on his face. He began to stutter, "Not to . . . not to—?"

"Yes," said Ruth, "to Billy Graham." He dived into the crowd and Ruth continued on, chuckling, but was also concerned that she hadn't been able to help him.

Interestingly enough, there was a painting on one of the walls in the home of Ruth's parents, Dr. and Mrs. Nelson Bell, called *The Restraining Hand.* It showed a large hand, representing God's, holding back a ravenous wolf from his planned attack on some helpless lambs. It was signed, "Ruth McCue Bell."

A little child told her grandmother, "You're not old; your skin still fits your face." Should it happen that Ruth's face ever becomes smocked with wrinkles so that the skin doesn't fit, it won't make any difference because, as someone has said, "The older we grow, the more like ourselves we become." This is the best possible news for those who are devoted to Ruth.

When one of the Gabor sisters was asked which of the Gabors was the oldest, she said, "Mother is, but she won't admit it." Ruth couldn't care less who knows her age.

A friend received a letter from Billy, written on January 2, 1960, in which he mentioned a cough which Ruth still has. An excerpt from the letter reads, "Now Ruth and I are going away for a few days in a sunny spot. As you perhaps know, she has had this serious cough for three months and the doctors have felt that she must get rid of it. Then I leave on the seventeenth for Africa." In closing, he asked for prayer for his meeting there.

The cough has cut down on Ruth's speaking engagements but, as she says, "One speaker in the family is enough." She felt this was especially true the day she failed to show up to speak to a group of women who had gathered to hear her. When she was finally located, she was found to be digging worms with their youngest son. She hadn't received the letter asking her to speak.

Besides having the persistent and aggravating cough, Ruth has also been plagued with an extremely painful arthritic hip, which recently involved a hip replacement requiring three operations. During that period of time she nearly lost her life.

Months before Ruth knew she would have to have the operation, an acquaintance, knowing Ruth's addiction to fun, told her that both she and her husband had arthritic hips and that since hers was the right hip and his was the left, they found they could conserve energy by taking to bed only one electric heating pad and putting it between them where it could take care of both her hip and his. She also reminded Ruth of the time Ruth had sent her flowers when she was in the hospital and had written on the card, "Get well or something."

Billy once said of Ruth, "I've never heard her complain." To my knowledge, neither has anyone else. A friend, using a little poetic license, said, "Ruth's head could be going around like a concrete mixer and her fever reach such heights that you'd need potholders to touch her forehead, and she'd ignore her condition and be concerned about a friend's hiccups."

In addition to the other medical problems, Ruth, who is usually as surefooted as a mountain goat, fell out of a tree when putting up a cable slide for her grandchildren. The result was a serious concussion which for a time affected her memory. The only concern Ruth seemed to have about her memory loss was the fact that the many Bible verses she'd stockpiled in her memory since childhood were gone. A staunch believer in the promise of God that "He is able to do exceeding abundantly above all that we ask or think," she continued to bombard heaven with her prayers until the verses were restored.

Years before, Ruth had written a friend that she was spending her time, while sunbathing, memorizing Bible verses. She commented on the fact that it was "the greatest source of refreshment that I know."

Ruth once said, "Time does not heal; only the Lord does."

When a certain person wondered aloud what Ruth could possibly find to occupy herself on top of the mountain except to watch television, a friend, knowing Ruth's habits, was incredulous. She had received a letter from Ruth saying, "There aren't enough hours in the day!"

One woman, when asked how she spent her time, said, "I'm a bench sitter with no compellments." Ruth isn't. She writes books, composes poems (already published in book form), writes a column for *Christianity Today*, and keeps up with many friends by letter and other ways. (She's also written twenty-five letters to one prisoner who, before her interest in him, was suicidal.) She speaks, for years taught a Sunday School class to college students, paints, sews, needlepoints, embroiders, braids rugs, cooks both simple and exotic meals, plays the piano, and raises gorgeous flowers as well as baby-sitting the grandchildren. She's also an amateur architect and has, in the past, even tackled and fixed "out of whack" plumbing. You name it—she can probably do it, and better than many. Her housemother at college said that she'd be a success at anything she undertook. She particularly mentioned her qualities of poise, courtesy, and forcefulness.

Ruth's father said of her, "If ever a person has wholly dedicated her life to God, Ruth has." (Even as a child, it showed. In a letter to Santa Claus written in her childish scrawl, she mentioned her concern for his spiritual life.)

Ruth doesn't plague you with a holier-than-thou attitude, and she recoils almost fiercely at the idea of being put on a pedestal. When she was told that certain people were doing just that, she said, "They aren't anymore." "Why?" she was asked. "They couldn't find one low enough," she grimaced.

One day a friend passed her on the mountain when she was driving the family jeep and mistakenly thought she was wearing a hat. Later, when she mentioned it, Ruth said resignedly, "It couldn't have been a hat; it must have been my halo." Then she added, "You know, a halo has to slip only a few inches to become a noose."

One of Ruth's daughters mentioned the fact that she'd seen tears in her mother's eyes only twice. I remember Ruth telling about her traumatic experience of leaving home at thirteen to go off to school in Korea and how she cried every night for three weeks because of homesickness, even asking God to let her die. Maybe Ruth "cried it out" at that time. Billy remarked of that period that God was preparing Ruth for "a lifetime of good-byes."

In any event, though few things now bring tears to Ruth's eyes, she's been able to bring tears to the eyes of many who have read her poem "Done with Play" from her book of poems, each of which gives an unparalleled glimpse into Ruth's very soul.

> I'm Daniel Creasman's mother
> I brung these clothes
> so's you
> could dress him up real natural like—
> no . . .
> navy wouldn't do.
>
> He liked this little play suit—
> it's sorta faded now—
> that tore place
> he got tryin'
> to help his Daddy plow.
> no . . .
> if he dressed real smart-like
> and all that fancy trim—
> the last we'd see of Danny,
> it wouldn't seem like him.
>
> But . . .
> comb his hair . . . real special
> (it wouldn't seem too odd) . . .

I brush it so, come Sunday
when he goes to the house of God.

That afternoon
I saw him—
so still, so tanned he lay—
with the faded blue suit on him
like he'd just come in from play . . .
but his hair was brushed
"real special"
and it didn't seem
one bit odd,
for . . .
he was just a small boy,
done with play
gone home to the house of God.[1]

For as long as anyone can remember, there's been a small water-spattered framed motto, the color of old dried bones, near Ruth's sink. It says to her and anyone looking, "PRAISE, PRAY, AND PEG AWAY." It was given to her when she told her parents good-bye and left on that momentous trip for school when she was thirteen. She's patterned her life by it.

Ruth has come as near as anyone I know to fulfilling the command of Christ to "Pray without ceasing." She calls prayer her "Continuing Conversation" with God.

Her impact on Billy, the children, friends, relatives, and the thousands of Mr. and Mrs. Creasmans and others whose lives she's been able to bless is due in great measure to the fact that her whole life is crisscrossed by prayer. From childhood, she has had daily audiences with the King of kings and Lord of lords, who uses earthly thrones as his footstools.

An overnight guest in the Graham home was quietly slipping out at daybreak. Tiptoeing down the hall, she glanced in the kitchen and, with the aid of the early fingers of dawn lighting the scene, she saw Ruth seated at the table with her head down on an open Bible. Ruth didn't hear her because her ears were tuned to God alone, around whom her entire life revolves.

Note

1. From Ruth Bell Graham, *Sitting by My Laughing Fire,* copyright © 1977 by Ruth Bell Graham; used by permission of Word Books, Publisher, Waco, Texas 76796.

4

Ruth's Parents

Before the death of Ruth's father, Dr. L. Nelson Bell, someone said to her, "I'd hate to have to choose between your husband and your father as to who is the greatest."

Some, without hesitation, would have chosen her father, and Billy himself would be among them.

At the Dallas crusade Billy introduced his father-in-law, Dr. Bell, as "the most unforgettable Christian I've ever known." Sixty thousand people rose in a standing ovation as this Christian saint was presented.

Dr. Bell and his wife lived in Montreat near the Grahams. After their deaths Bunny, their granddaughter, said, "They don't make people like them anymore."

In the foreword of the book *A Foreign Devil in China*, which is the story of Dr. Bell's life, Billy's comments leave no doubt as to the love and respect he and countless others felt for his father-in-law.

Billy goes on to say that his father-in-law, having been forced by circumstances to leave his missionary activities in China, returned to the United States to find his Presbyterian church divided and in a state of theological confusion.

Consequently, as soon as was possible, he took time out from a heavy schedule as a surgeon to found the *Presbyterian Journal,* and later joined with others in founding *Christianity Today*—in time becoming its executive editor.

Billy said of *Christianity Today* that in the preceding ten years, it had influenced more clergymen than any other magazine. (It continues to expand in subscriptions and influence.)

Billy further stated that the writings coming from Dr. Bell's pen were read not only by the clergy but by Christians the world over.

(Joking about the *Presbyterian Journal* and its forthright, fearless printing of and comments about the news, a friend of Dr. Bell's, chuckling, said, "The *New York Times* prints all the news that's 'fit' to print. Certain other papers, all the news that 'fits', they print. The *Journal,* all the news that 'gives fits,' it prints.")

The *Presbyterian Journal* has as its editor Dr. Aiken Taylor, who worked hand in hand with Dr. Bell and Dr. Henry Dendy for some years and under whose watchful eye the *Journal* has continued to grow and expand. As someone gratefully said concerning the *Journal,* "No insult to God or the Bible goes unchallenged."

Dr. Bell gave as his reason for founding the *Journal* the fact that in his church the conservative voice had been all but strangled.

Some years ago, out of a heart full of love and concern for his beloved church, Dr. Bell wrote a significant book expressing his concerns and the dangers facing the church. It was titled *While Men Slept.* Some who have read it have compared it with the concerns expressed by Richard G. Hutchenson in his hard-hitting and widely read book, *Mainline Churches and The Evangelicals.*

They see in both the sown seed and its resulting fruit. Many see in Hutchenson's book a vindication of Dr. Bell and his anxieties.

Numerous readers feel that the thing that lifts Hutchenson's book from the area of nonsense scribbling (which might have been the case if a conservative had written it) is his divulging the fact that his entire background has been "liberal-ecumenical."

Numerous people have suggested cures for the state of the church. If Dr. Bell has been read aright, he would offer as an instant cure an inerrant Bible.

Dr. Bell used to say of himself that in his church, he acted as the burr under the saddle. He was also a man of unlimited courage and has been heard to say, "A man shouldn't wear out three pairs of pants straddling the fence."

His honors were enviable. He was elected moderator of the General Assembly of his church, the highest office available. In competition with newsmen from all over the nation, he was eight times given the Freedom Award from Valley Forge. He was twice investigated by the IRS; it was difficult for the auditors to understand how he could give so much money to charitable causes. (He got a clean bill of health.) On Sunday mornings he taught a radio Bible class with a potential of thirty thousand listeners. The L. Nelson Bell Library at Montreat Anderson College (Christian) was built in his honor. He was a baseball pro in the days before God called him as a medical missionary to China, where he served as head surgeon in the largest Presbyterian hospital there.

Dr. Bell was one of the most endearing personalities of his time, even gaining respect from those who disagreed violently with him. He never backed off from controversial subjects but always told the truth in love. Comments such as this have been heard since his death: "Montreat and the church will never be the same without him." Ruth, like others, still remembers the *little* things. Not too long ago I heard her say pensively, "I wish I hadn't bought him that new bed. I think he missed his old one." Someone called him "God's own"—a warm, loving, and witty person. When he was around seventy-seven years of age someone remarked that he looked fifty-five. "That old?" he asked, his brow furrowing.

When he was asked how it would be possible for anyone to get down the very steep driveway leading to a friend's house, he said, "You ski in and come out on crutches." At seventy-seven he was still bouncing up and down the basement stairs that led to his office. However, because he was plagued with a bad heart, a chairlift finally had to be installed.

Dr. Bell loved people. If a neighbor were ill, he'd fix a delectable casserole and trudge through the snow to put it on her table. For twenty-four years he and "Ginny," his wife, drove every Sunday afternoon to visit a friend in a nursing home, a round trip of probably fifty miles or more.

When Ginny herself developed arthritis and had to be confined to a wheelchair, he became her nurse as well as holding on to his other jobs. In a letter to one of their daughters he wrote, "She's so precious to take care of."

Ginny was an unusual person in her own right. When Ruth had to be away from the children, she stood in the gap, giving them love, care, discipline, and spiritual guidance.

Ruth said, "Mother never asked me what I could do for her; it was always, 'Ruth, what can I do for you?'"

She apparently had no fear. Before she was confined to the wheelchair, she drove her own car. I'm reminded of an eighty-year-old woman I knew in a retirement home who was like her in her fearlessness. She would drive the residents to and from the airport, fifty miles away. On this particular day she was speeding in order to get her passenger to the plane on time. A motorcycle policeman finally caught up with her. As he drew alongside, she stuck her head out of the window and told him, "Don't stop me now. I'll talk to you later." He let her go—was probably too stunned to do anything else.

It was recalled that Ginny would be in a long line of cars whose drivers were scared to pass the police car at the head of the line. She would gun her engine, dart out of line, and pass the police car, almost drawing it in her back window as she went by. A friend commented, "I wouldn't be surprised to see her scratch off in her wheelchair the same way."

After Dr. Bell's death, Ruth took her mother into their home and cared for her until, propelled by her independent spirit, she moved back into her own home. Some were reminded of the time Billy was on a platform with a comedian who had jokingly said that when his parents got old he was going to put them in a home. Billy said, "I hope it will be *your* home," or a similar response.

Because death is so much a part of life and, for the Christian, the beginning of a glorious eternal existence in heaven, the Graham children weren't kept from attending funerals. Chris, Ruth's secretary, told of taking one of their black friends to a funeral. Little Bunny went along and Chris said, "Bunny had never been to a funeral before, so she wanted to sit in the car. However, by the time she saw all the activities, the beautiful flowers being carried inside the church, the Sunday clothes everyone wore, and the way the relatives and friends were hugging and loving one another, she became enthusiastic about funerals and said she could hardly wait for another funeral to take place so she could attend."

That night Bunny was especially concerned over the health of Dr. and Mrs. Bell, who were not feeling well. As she concluded her prayers, she said, "And please, Jesus, don't let Niang and Loi die" (their Chinese names). Then hopping back into bed, she pulled the covers up to her chin and cheerfully exclaimed, "But if they do, I'll go to the funeral."

An internationally known speaker and writer had arrived in Montreat to speak at a church conference. He mentioned to a friend that he had just seen Dr. Bell and that he didn't look well.

He was then told, "When Dr. Bell called you to ask you to speak at this conference, he had pulled the table phone under the oxygen tent in the hospital, where he was being treated for a severe heart attack."

A story is told about an elderly doctor who was called one night by a young man who wanted him to make a house call on his wife, who had been taken ill. When the doctor asked if the caller could pay him, the young man responded rather indignantly that he could. The old doctor asked, "Then would you mind calling a younger doctor? I only go out at night for those who can't afford to pay." It could have been Dr. Bell speaking.

5

With This Ring

Though nearly everyone else calls him Billy, Ruth calls him Bill. "Me call that big thing Billy?" she asks.

Since their marriage, Billy has been gone from home so much of the time that some have seriously wondered if Ruth had ever had any regrets about marrying him. Some have even left the impression that Ruth might be calling from their mountain home, "Help! I'm being held against my will!"

Ruth has laid this concern to rest many times, the first time in Glasgow, Scotland, many years ago. She told a Boston reporter, "I want you to know that I'd rather have Billy Graham part time than anybody else in the world full time." And probably too many times to count, she's given the classic answer, "I'd rather see a little of him than a lot of any other man."

Years ago she wrote a friend, "I'd be bored to death with any other man." And again, "Don't our husbands know how much they mean to us and how much we love them? Neither of us would be worth a plugged nickel without them." And then, in irrepressible gratitude, "Hasn't the Lord been good to us?"

Almost since childhood, Ruth's plan was to go to Tibet as a missionary. There are those who wonder out loud if she's ever regretted her decision to not go. The answer: She feels it was God's decision, not hers.

Backpedaling to Wheaton College days: Ruth tells that one Sunday she was in a room where the Sunday School teachers gathered to pray before they left for their assignments in town. The men and women met in separate rooms. Ruth said, "All of a sudden I heard a voice from the next room. I had never heard anyone pray that way before. I knew that someone was talking to God. It seemed that here was a man who knew God in a very unusual way." It was Billy.

Soon after that, she met Billy. From the first he was hopelessly and incurably in love with her. He wrote his mother that he'd just met the most beautiful girl on campus and was going to marry her. Then, he admits, he went into a period of deep depression, feeling that there was nothing about him good enough to offer her.

But Ruth was having thoughts of her own about Billy. Though with her, it wasn't exactly love at first sight, it wasn't long before she knelt beside her bed and said inaudibly to God that if she could spend the rest of her life serving him with Billy, she'd consider it the greatest privilege imaginable.

Did Billy meet the qualifications Ruth had told God she wanted in a husband? Many years before she met Billy, she had put her hopes in a prayer poem to God:

> Dear God, I prayed, all unafraid
> (as we're inclined to do)
> I do not need a handsome man
> But let him be like You;
> I do not need one big and strong nor yet so very tall,

> nor need he be some genius,
> or wealthy, Lord, at all;
> but let his head be high, dear God,
> and let his eye be clear,
> his shoulders straight, whate'er his state,
> whate'er his earthly sphere;
> and let his face have character,
> a ruggedness of soul,
> and let his whole life show, dear God,
> a singleness of goal;
> then, when he comes,
> (as he will come)
> with quiet eyes aglow,
> I'll understand that he's the man
> I prayed for, long ago.[1]

When some people match the poem to the man, they have the feeling that nothing happens in a moment of God's absentmindedness. One of Ruth's favorite Bible verses is, "Trust in the Lord with all thine heart; and lean not unto thine understanding. In all thy ways acknowledge him, and he shall direct thy paths" (Prov. 3:56).

Because the change in Ruth's plan to go to Tibet seemed so drastic to her, she felt she needed even more assurance from God that he was giving her the "go ahead." Like Gideon in the Bible, she figuratively put out the fleece (Judg. 6:37-40). The sign that she asked God to give was a simple one. She was to ask Billy if he believed in signs and, if God approved of Ruth's change of plans, Billy was to thrust his hands into his pockets. He did. (Ruth doesn't remember this, but others do.)

Ruth had her answer, but she admitted that if she'd had an inkling as to what was ahead of her as the wife of Billy Graham, she'd have been terrified.

It's a well-known fact that Billy was once turned down by a lovely girl who wanted to marry someone who would "amount to something." Ruth's appraisal of her is "Cute as a button."

Some years ago, Ruth told the then-grown son of this woman, "The nicest thing your dad ever did for me was to marry your mother." When the son met the older Graham daughter for the first time, he quipped, "Just think, you might have been me!"

On hearing that Billy was engaged to Ruth, a friend of his commented to Billy that he was marrying a "little mountain girl." So Ruth impishly got ready for Billy's first visit to her home to meet her parents.

She put on an old faded dress that looked like a Salvation Army reject and didn't fit anywhere, then let down her hair, blacked out a front tooth, and went barefoot down the road to meet him. When Billy's car came into sight, Ruth called to him. She said he pushed the accelerator to the floorboards and took off like a scared rabbit, with her running down the road behind the car shouting, ungrammatically, "It's me, Bill."

Ruth's little brother, Clayton, called her engagement ring a "grindstone!" (He is now the minister of the largest Presbyterian church in the United States.)

Some time after Ruth graduated from Wheaton, she was in a room in Montreat, sewing. A man came in and said, "What fool girl is going to be married on Friday the thirteenth?" Ruth, deftly jabbing the needle into the wedding dress she was making, admitted, "I am."

Ruth's prayer before she and Billy were married:

> God,
> let me be all he ever dreamed

of loveliness and laughter,
Veil his eyes a bit
because
there are so many little flaws;
somehow, God,
please let him see
only the bride I long to be,
remembering ever after—
I was all he ever dreamed
of loveliness and laughter.[2]

Anyone who knows Ruth is confident that her prayer was answered.

In another poem, Ruth put down the memories of their wedding—expressed in bell-toned words which chime out the beautiful thoughts that one has come to expect from Ruth.

With this ring . . .
your strong, familiar voice
fell like a benediction
on my heart, that dusk,
tall candles flickered gently
Our age-old vows were said,
and I could hear
someone begin to sing
an old, old song,
timeworn and lovely,
timeworn and dear.
And in that dusk
were old, old friends
and you,
an old friend, too
(and dearer than them all)
Only my ring seemed new-

its plain gold
surface
warm and bright
and strange to me
that candlelight . . .
unworn-unmarred
Could it be that wedding rings
like other things,
are lovelier when scarred?[3]

Life shuttles between the serious and the lighthearted. No life could bear the burden of sustained solemnity or sustained merriment. So we cry. So we laugh.

Billy laughs at memories of their honeymoon at Blowing Rock, North Carolina. He says one dinner cost so much that his honeymoon budget was in a shambles and they had to pack up and leave early.

In recent years, Billy has been spoken of as the "Aging Lion of Evangelism." Ruth approves, saying that his face is much more interesting now that it has character lines in it. And since Billy has at times said that he wished the Lord would call him home, he realizes that the sprinkling of gray in his hair and the gentle lines in his face are indicative of the fact that he's continuing his journey down the home stretch—to his eternal home.

But to some observers, it looks like it's going to be a slow journey because Billy, who looks on his body as the temple of the Holy Spirit, takes excellent care of it. He continues to watch his diet and faithfully exercises, which includes jogging. An observer says, "I wouldn't say Billy can outrun a cheetah, but he leaves his jogging partners behind, panting like fish on a carpet."

After Billy came into public prominence, his height, wavy golden hair, piercing blue eyes, and tanned skin made him the target of even a movie studio which offered him a screen test.

At one of his earlier crusades, a staff member was seated behind two women. At the conclusion of Billy's sermon, one of the ladies turned to her companion and asked, "Well, what do you think of what he had to say?" Her friend replied, "Honey, I didn't come to listen to him. I came to look at him."

For years, Ruth has refused to let me tell this, saying, "Bill would hate it"; but since I think their attitude is an excellent indication of what they consider important, I'm telling it, hoping that she'll relent and that I won't have to be taken into protective custody

Ruth is slimmer now than when she and Billy met. She once said, "Bill hates fat." Perhaps the fact that she is allergic to some foods has also helped to keep her weight down, but the main thing she has going for her is that she doesn't have an "overactive fork." Consequently, she doesn't have to remove her bobby pins when she weighs.

Billy can never hope to find words to express to the world his true feelings about Ruth. He's often said that their marriage is a heaven on earth, and he gives the credit to Ruth. He recognizes the fact, as do many others, that Ruth was handpicked by God, himself, to be his wife. Ruth has had far more than a "bit" part in the drama of Billy's life.

Not everyone feels about his wife as Billy does. One man wrote Billy a letter, the gist of which was that he loved his wife and they got along fine, but that he just didn't see how he'd be able to put up with her through all eternity. Billy was able to relieve his mind by telling him that Christ had said that there would be no marriage in heaven.

An article in *Christianity Today* said about Billy, "His wife, Ruth, offers sound counsel and provides a stabilizing counterbalance, and his close friends have concluded that half of what Billy is has come through his wife."

Not surprisingly, one columnist wrote that Ruth, a Presbyterian, was the most important person in Billy's life. He added that Billy not only admired her selection in clothes, but depended on her for criticism and almost never failed to take her advice.

One columnist wrote that Billy "married gloriously." He said he couldn't understand why Billy was so concerned with the devil when he had such an angel at home.

John Pollock in the book *Billy Graham* gives Ruth the credit for broadening Billy. He mentions her interest in and love of art and literature and the fact that she'd had the opportunity to travel. He seemed particularly impressed by the realization that it was Ruth who had kept alive in Billy a portion of the little boy, who, without her influence, might have developed into a person whose seriousness bordered on stuffiness.

On his well-known talk show, David Frost tried to pin Billy down regarding his "possessions." He asked a hypothetical question as to which of Billy's possessions he'd like for a burglar to leave behind when burglarizing his house. Billy answered without hesitation: "My wife!" The audience cheered.

Thankfully, in the following poem, we feel we have come across the tears that we were afraid were no longer being shed. The tears Ruth sheds make her a kindred spirit to us who also cry:

> Love
> without clinging;

cry—
if you must—
but privately cry;
the heart will adjust
to the newness of loving
in practical ways;
cleaning
and cooking
and sorting out clothes,
all say, "I love you"
when lovingly done.

So—
love
without clinging.
cry—
if you must—
but privately cry;
the heart will adjust
to the length of his stride,
the song he is singing,
the trail he must ride,
the tensions that make him
the man that he is,
the world he must face,
the life that is his.

So—
love
without clinging;
cry—
if you must—
but privately cry;
the heart will adjust
to being the heart,
not the forefront of life;
a part of himself,

not the object—
his wife.
So—
love![4]

For some reason, the sky seems to wait for Billy to arrive home to start a downpour.

Billy admits to some depression when he's in gloomy, rainy weather for too long a time. A friend commented, "A few drops of rain falling on Billy makes him think he's been standing in a car wash."

Ruth reminds you of Elijah's servant who could spot a cloud in the sky when it was the size of a man's hand. She says, "Billy can spot one even before it's that size."

One day the sun's rays were coming down through the leaves of the trees, littering the ground with swatches of sunlight and gushing into the Graham home—one of those luminous blonde days. Ruth heard Billy's voice saying with joyous abandon, "This is the day the Lord hath made."

Some days later, the earth was ash gray, dreary, and soggy from rain. There was a significant silence from Billy's room, so Ruth stuck her head in the door and reminded him, "This is also the day that the Lord hath made."

Has the Graham marriage been one of continuous bliss and ecstasy with no arguments or disagreements? Those who can't say that of their own marriage were grateful for the boost Ruth gave them on the Donahue Show. When he asked Ruth if she'd ever considered divorce, she said, deadpan, "Divorce, never—murder many times." When she was asked if she ever disagreed with Billy, she said, "Not with my hair in curlers."

As always, Ruth's innermost thoughts come to the surface in her poems:

> You look at me
> and see
> my flaws;
> I look at you
> and see flaws, too.
> Those who love,
> know love
> deserves a second glance;
> each failure serves
> another chance.
> Love looks to see
> beyond the scars
> and flaws,
> the cause;
> and scars become
> an honorable badge
> of battles fought
> and won—
> (or lost)
> but fought!
> The product
> not the cost
> is what love sought.
>
> God help us see
> beyond the now
> to the before,
> and note with
> tenderness
> what lies between
> —and love the more.[5]

Also, for those couples who feel that their marriages have insurmountable problems, Ruth holds out hope as she candidly gives in her book *It's My Turn* the details of their first major disagreement. Ruth says this is how it ended: "Kneeling beside the overstuffed chair, tears pouring furiously down my face, I prayed, 'Lord, if you'll forgive me for marrying him, I'll never do it again.'"[6]

Of course she concludes that it was "undoubtedly the dumbest prayer I ever prayed." And she goes on to say that Billy later realized how thoughtless he'd been and made abject apologies.

But for couples who had thought the Graham marriage was nothing short of perfection, therefore out of reach, Ruth's words will probably prove to be a great relief.

In speaking of love, the last verse of one of Ruth's poems expresses the hopes of many married couples:

> Deepen it
> throughout the years;
> age and mellow it
> until
> time that finds us
> old without,
> within,
> will find us lovers still.[7]

Because of the boxcar headlines, tickertape, and flashbulb existence, a friend once asked Ruth if she thought Billy would ever succumb to pride (the sin that's highest on the list in the criminal files of heaven). Ruth said thoughtfully, "No, I don't think so. Billy is always conscious of that temptation and stays on his knees about it. Satan will try to get him where he least expects it."

An editorial in *Christianity Today* said: "Graham moves in circles to which few evangelists have access. He is at home with the press, a hard-bitten and cynical fraternity of men who can expose a phony in short order. Graham has a remarkable ability to handle sensitive questions and sidestep booby traps. He has been wined

and dined by presidents and royalty, but public prominence has left him seemingly unchanged and humble."

In line with the above statement, a friend reports that
she and several others were in the Graham living room
with Billy one day. She confesses that she was thun-
derstruck at the way this man who, from all eternity, has
had an appointment with greatness, burrowed under the
reticence of a young man present and got him to talk
about himself. To the listeners, the young man was made
to appear ten feet tall while Billy receded into the
background by choice.

A mutual friend of Billy's and mine recently told me of
an occasion when he and several golfing partners were on
their way out of the club dining room with Billy. A young
girl stopped Billy and asked, "Dr. Graham, would you
please give me your autograph?" Billy smiled and said,
"Yes, if you'll give me yours."

Ruth is also a very humble person who tries to lead
people away from the fame circuit. When Billy's now-
famous radio program first went on the air, it was Ruth
who defeated the high-pressure advertising men who
wanted to use Billy's name in the title. She suggested
calling it "The Hour of Decision."

Someone once said of Billy, "Some people look on him
almost as God." This is terrifying to both Billy and Ruth.
They're always conscious of Peter's words in Acts
10:25-26; the angel's words in Revelation 19:10; the account of Herod's death because he accepted the glory that
was God's, Acts 12:21-23; and God's words, "My glory will
I not give to another" (Isa. 42:8). One of Ruth's favorite
hymns is, "To God Be the Glory."

After observing Ruth for many years, I feel safe in

saying that I think her prayer for Billy would go something like this: "Thank you, God, that you have used him in such a powerful way as a challenger of Satan. Thank you for his character, his pleasing personality, and his appearance. Now blot him out and let the people see only you."

Much of the respect that people continue to have for Billy stems from the fact that he's quick to confess his sins and failures. He's often told the vast crowds, "Keep your eyes on Christ, not on me. I'll fail you every time."

It's said that the devil gets out a special edition when a saint goes wrong, so Billy has been scrupulously careful to avoid even "the appearance of evil," as the Bible says. He's even refused to ride in the car with his secretary unless some of the staff is with him. But even so, Ruth tells of a newspaper in Eastern Europe which was out to get Billy's scalp and reported once that he was seen in a tavern in the company of a blonde girl, drinking. But they also reported the blonde's name, "Beverly Shea." (For those who don't know, Bev has been the male singer for the crusade since its inception.) Ruth wrote home, "Give them enough rope and they'll hang themselves." A further comment from her was that at the time of the news report, "He was in the hospital suffering from a kidney stone attack." God says, "Blessed are ye, when men shall revile you, and persecute you, and shall say all manner of evil against you falsely, for my sake. Rejoice, and be exceeding glad: for great is your reward in heaven" (Matt. 5:11-12).

The Bible doesn't hesitate to wash the soiled linen of the saints in public, and Billy and Ruth seem to measure up better than many of the biblical saints.

An article in *Christianity Today* said of Billy, "God ordered that the gospel is to be preached by men, not angels. Billy Graham is a man with all the explosive potential that the image of God makes possible. He's subject to all the human frailties all of us experience. He has come to his mature years transparent in his life, charismatic, open, highly likable. Those who oppose him can't deny that he is a Christian, infused with the radiant spirit of the love of Christ. He is a veteran crusader, unflappable, very much at home in his role as evangelist."

When Grady Wilson (a staff member) was being rolled into the operating room, Billy told him, "When you're under ether, confess your sins but don't confess mine."

Actually, Ruth once told me that "God got to him before too much damage was done." And a person who knows Billy well said that if Billy had been a member of a church that had a confessional, his sins would have been so boring they would have closed it down. But not so, according to God's Word, which says that if we sin in one point, we are guilty of all (Jas. 2:10).

There have been the crepe hangers who have continued to predict that Billy was washed up and on his way out, but their predictions are about as accurate as the crochety traveling preacher who told Billy at twelve, "Run along, little fellow. You'll never be a preacher."

Billy said in an interview in *Christianity Today*, "I didn't think there would be that much interest, but we have more invitations from all over the world than we can take in two lifetimes."

On one occasion Ruth was asked about the report that Billy was quitting evangelism. When asked the source of the report, she was told it was on the radio several times the preceding day. She said, "He'll quit when he's under six feet of earth." When she was asked who could have started the rumor, she said, "His enemies."

Billy settled the question once for all in an interview in *Christianity Today*. He said, "So long as God gives me strength, I will continue—maybe I can continue until I am seventy. But it is all in God's hand . . . I feel better now than I did in my forties when I tried to do too much."

In another poem from her book of poems, *Sitting by My Laughing Fire*, Ruth speaks of her husband's arms as being her home. A reader is able to plumb the depths of her feelings in the many other poems that reflect the joys and sorrows of the life that she and Billy have made together.

Ruth rather recently said, "After thirty-five years of marriage, you really begin to understand the richness of love"—and that hers and Billy's love now is deeper than they had ever dreamed it could be. Billy mentioned the fact that the children seemed concerned that he and Ruth were all alone on the mountain, now that they were gone. Billy said, "We're having the time of our lives," and spoke of sitting in the rocking chairs on the porch, holding hands, sometimes talking and sometimes not, but often able to tell what the other one was thinking without the intrusion of words.

In the following poem, a reader has a glimpse into the joyous life that has been theirs in Ruth's heartfelt cry to God—written about her as a bride but probably even more meaningful after thirty-five years of marriage:

> Never let it end, God
> never-please
> all the growing loveliness,
> all of these
> brief moments of
> fresh pleasure—
> never let it end.

Let us always
be a little
breathless at love's beauty,
never let us
stop to measure
just how much to give;
never let us
stoop to weigh love;
let us live—
and live!
Please God,
let our hearts kneel always,
Love their only Master,
Knowing the warm impulsiveness
of shattered alabaster.
I know you can see things
the way a new bride sees,
so
never let it end, God,
Never, please.[8]

Notes

1-5. From Ruth Bell Graham, *Sitting by My Laughing Fire,*
copyright © 1977 by Ruth Bell Graham; used by permission of
Word Books, Publisher, Waco, Texas 76796.

6. From *It's My Turn* by Ruth Bell Graham copyright © 1982
by Ruth Bell Graham. Published by Fleming H. Revell Company. Used by permission.

7-8. From Ruth Bell Graham, *Sitting by My Laughing Fire,*
copyright © 1977 by Ruth Bell Graham; used by permission of
Word Books, Publisher, Waco, Texas 76796.

6

Ruth as Mother

Although Ruth has been in demand as a speaker for Presidential Prayer Breakfasts (Women's Section), radio and television interviews, and the recipient of national awards and platform speaker, the role she loves best is, as she said in a recent letter, "to be the wife, homemaker and *grandmother* I need to be—that God called me to be."

Being a grandmother is an ongoing process of being a mother, which Ruth has always said was the greatest calling on earth. And after seeing how the children have turned out, observers would agree that as a mother, Ruth has won her spurs.

She was more than qualified for her role as mother; she was mature long before her time due to experiences in China when she was a child. She tells of finding one live girl baby, with its eyes closed with pus but still alive, who had been abandoned by her parents. A Chinese woman cradled it in her arms and rushed with it to the hospital where Ruth's Dad was the chief surgeon, but she was too late. The baby died. Ruth even tells of seeing dogs tearing one baby apart.

The Graham children were surrounded by love. After

they were fed, bathed, and ready for bed, one would say, "It's lovin' time," and they'd all rush pell mell toward Ruth, piling on her lap and climbing on the back and arms of her chair. They smothered their mother with hugs and kisses, which were enthusiastically returned.

The children loved Ruth's tales about "the olden days" when she was a child, but it was hard for them to accept some of the primitive practices she had to live through such as being bathed in the same water her sisters and brothers had been bathed in. They didn't see how anyone could get squeaky clean in dirty bath water. (Many oldsters living today can also remember bathing in "used" bath water, I for one.)

At times, Ruth has given the impression that she feels a wistful nostalgia for the days when life was so much simpler. When their first child was a baby, Ruth had only one baby-sitter that she could count on (except her mother). Sometimes Ruth would have to go to her mother's house, which was across the street, but too far away to leave the sleeping baby unattended. So she'd call the lone telephone operator, a friend, and tell her she was pulling the baby's crib under the wall telephone and putting the receiver in the crib; and if the baby made a sound, she could call her at her mother's and she'd head for home on the run.

Ruth took motherhood in her stride and was very comfortable with it. She was "easy going." If the children wanted to hang onto their bottles after the so-called acceptable time to give them up, it was all right with her. (I once piously told my doctor brother-in-law whose five-year-old child was still drinking out of a bottle, "I certainly wouldn't fix a bottle for a five-year-old child." He said, "We don't; he fixes his own.") So did the Graham children; however, when they felt they were too old to be using bottles, if a visitor was in the room, they'd skitter by the guest sideways like crabs, holding the bottles under the folds of their nightgowns.

After Ruth had heard their prayers and tucked them in bed for the night, she'd tie up the day's loose ends, have her own devotions, and finally get to bed. However, that didn't mean that she'd get to stay there because her mother ear was always cocked to hear the slightest sound from a child.

I remember that on one occasion she was up in the night, scrambling on all fours to find for a sobbing child an escaped cricket he'd taken to bed with him in a Bandaid box.

That experience led her to tell of a traumatic experience of her own childhood when she'd gone to bed with a baby duck, rolled over on it in the night, and killed it.

Ruth holds to the cherished mementos of the children's childhood—both physical and verbal.

The little crude cross made of twigs which hangs on the wall in her room was made for her by Franklin when he was a tiny boy—and I feel confident that Ruth would try to brave smoke and flame to rescue it. "Down at the Cross" was Franklin's favorite hymn when he was a child.

The Graham household didn't escape the little nagging problems common to all households. Ruth, who is usually as neat as a new spring suit, waked up later than usual one morning and, being pressed for time, hurried to the kitchen without fixing her face or combing her hair. She picked up the baby who had spit up his milk and was smelling unpleasantly sour. The three-year-old was on a crying jag. Ruth quickly fixed breakfast and put it on the table, then noticed that the seven-year-old was dawdling with her food. When she asked her the reason, GiGi threw down her fork and said, "Between lookin' at you, listenin' to Bunny, and smellin' Franklin, I've lost my appetite."

Ruth is a wonderful cook, and no one else that I know of has ever lost an appetite at her table. A woman who had met Ruth only a short time before tells of answering an early morning knock on her door and finding the three little Graham girls standing there with a note from their mother saying that she was fixing breakfast for her and her family. At the time, not knowing about Ruth's warm hospitality which often became evident in spur-of-the-moment invitations, she protested that it was too much of an imposition. GiGi and her sisters insisted vehemently that if she didn't come, their mother would have to throw out all the food. So the lady, feeling very fortunate, invited the children into the house to wait until they could get dressed to go. The little girls followed her into the kitchen and watched her turn off the stove under the corned beef hash she was fixing for breakfast. When they reached home, GiGi whispered excitedly to her mother, with accusing glances at their guest, that she'd been fixing dog food for her children's breakfast.

Most people would agree that a little child can make shambles of a wedding if she sets her mind to it. Ruth agrees.

I attended one wedding that both Ruth and little Bunny were in. Ruth was a bride's attendant, and Bunny was one of the flower girls. It turned into a suspenseful evening, with everyone wondering what the little pixie would do next to upstage the bride. Ruth preferred to just forget the whole thing until a psychiatrist, who was a guest, told her that her child's actions were those of a perfectly normal three-year-old.

First of all, Bunny started down the "bridal path" ahead of time and had to be retrieved. When she finally got to the platform, she had a slight altercation with the other flower girl as to where she was to stand. When she was convinced that she'd found her chalk mark, she jumped on it with both feet. Then, alarmed that she might not be on dead center, she leaned over in all directions, trying to see past her long dress to the mark. Finally, teetering to the point of almost losing her balance and doing a head stand, she pulled up her dress, then tried to look over the bunched dress material in her hands. When she was convinced she was on target, she blithely ignored the mark for the rest of the ceremony, prancing here and there among the members of the bridal party. Then she spotted a friend in the church, cupped her hands, and gently hallooed to her. Receiving no response, she wandered over to her mother and began taking her bouquet apart (while her mother was probably resisting the desire to take her apart). Her beleaguered mother finally got a firm hold on her wrist and Bunny said loudly, "Don't pinch me, Mamma." Ruth denied pinching her but didn't deny wanting to. A good time was had by all.

Speaking of long wedding dresses: One day the three little Graham girls had picked water lilies out of a small pond on Montreat property without asking permission, so Ruth told them they'd have to go to the authorities to confess. She told them to change their clothes, so they hurried upstairs and were back down in a few minutes dressed in the long dresses they'd worn in weddings (with an eye to swaying the jury, Ruth said). She sent them back up again. In a short time they were down, dressed sensibly, but carrying several clean dresses apiece, on hangers. When Ruth asked them the reason for the extra dresses, they told her that they'd probably have to go to jail and would need clean clothes. Ruth lowered her voice and said to a friend, "Let them boil in their own oil for a while."

After a particularly hectic time with the children, Ruth wrote a friend: "I've threatened to write a sequel to Bill's book *Peace With God*. Only this will be about our family and called *No Peace Here*."

At the last Fourth of July parade in the small community where the Graham children grew up, Anne and Bunny and their children were back on a visit and their children were in the parade.

Arriving in time to view the parade and noting that the children were having such a good time, Anne's husband remarked to me that he couldn't understand why his wife and the other Graham children hadn't taken part in the traditional parade when they were little. On reflecting on his remark, it was easy for me to come up with the answer. Ruth had succeeded in making the home such an enticing and fulfilling spot that the children didn't have to be kept in leg irons to keep them at home.

An entry in Ruth's diary from her book *It's My Turn* speaks of the times when child rearing is difficult:
"Things have not been going smoothly. There is a terrible amount of fighting among the children . . . and peevishness on my part, backed by sporadic, uncertain discipline.

"I am not walking the Lord's way at all. I am doing what I want to do rather than what I ought to do."

She further confesses, "I lie awake nights loathing myself for the person I am, fearful and worried that I cannot bring up this family as I should. And I can't."[1]

But these confessions are only a small part of the story. As always, when Ruth finds herself unable to cope with a situation, she calls on God to help, knowing that "God is our refuge and strength, a very present help in trouble"

(Ps. 46:1), and that when he enters the picture, the outlook is going to change.

Jesus loved the little children so much that he said, "Except ye be converted, and become as little children, ye shall not enter into the kingdom of heaven" (Matt. 18:3). He also said, "Take heed that ye despise not one of these little ones; for I say unto you, That in heaven their angels do always behold the face of my Father which is in heaven" (Matt. 18:10).

Years ago I read that when Jesus made the statement, "We have piped unto you and ye have not danced; we have mourned unto you and ye have not lamented," he was recalling a childhood rhyme connected with a game he'd played as a child on the streets of Nazareth. Children were so much a part of Christ's ministry. Using a child as an illustration, he said, "Whosoever therefore shall humble himself as this little child, the same is greatest in the kingdom of heaven" (Matt. 18:4). He also made a frightening statement concerning anyone who would cause a child to stumble: "But whoso shall offend one of these little ones which believe in me, it were better for him that a millstone were hanged about his neck, and that he were drowned in the depth of the sea" (Matt. 18:6).

It goes without saying that Billy and Ruth respected and followed such Scriptures as they raised their children. It has been said that when a child is old enough to love his mother, he is old enough to love God. Anne Graham says she felt a love of God at three.

Note

1. From *It's My Turn* by Ruth Bell Graham copyright © 1982 by Ruth Bell Graham. Published by Fleming H. Revell Company. Used by permission.

7

The Children's Sayings

Ruth's days were made richer by the children's sometimes sublime and sometimes comical expressions and reactions.

Franklin, at five, was an outdoors man. When he announced to his mother that he was going to spend the night outside, she reminded him of the roaming polecats. He then showed her his gun, which was to be his protector. Ruth said, "But Franklin, it's only a play gun." Franklin said, "The polecats don't know that."

Ruth was sometimes floored by his lack of inhibitions. One day they parked next to a couple at a drive-in movie theater showing a Disney-type picture. Franklin had been learning all about sanitation and germs in the first grade at school. When he saw the couple kissing, he stuck his head out of the window and called out, "Mister, you'd better watch out or you'll get germs from that lady of yours!" Ruth said she wanted to climb in the glove compartment.

One day when he was a small boy, a friend of Ruth's was taking care of him and he had a full-fledged nosebleed. It looked to her as though he were losing a pint of blood a minute, so she was flying around frantically trying to stem the flow. Nothing helped. She got more and more excited and said out loud to herself, "What will I *do*?" Franklin, bored, said, "Get a Bandaid."

Trying to describe one of his classmates to Ruth, he told her, "It's that boy that combs his hair."

Anne had her own picturesque way of describing things she observed. She called a bud "a flower that hasn't growed up yet." One day she was walking with an older friend and saw cucumbers growing. She said excitedly, "Look at the little pickles on the vine." When the children were little, there was usually a cow grazing near the Montreat gate which the children called, "Mrs. Cow." One day, Anne, concerned, told her mother, "He lowered his thorns at me." She referred to the doctor as "inspecting his patient."

One day Bunny was having a dinner in the home of a woman she'd just met. After a full meal, a large dish of sherbet was put before her. Not wanting to hurt her hostess's feelings, but knowing she couldn't eat it all, she leaned over to an older friend sitting next to her and whispered, "Would you mind takin' a handful of my sherbet?"

When Dale Evans's book *Angel Unaware* came off the press, one of the children said, "I didn't know that angels wore underwear." And of course, the "Acts of the Apostles" was "Axe of the Apostles."

One of Ruth's little nephews, the son of her sister, Virginia, said he liked ginger ale except for the "freckles" in it and the fact that it "spit" at him.

Little GiGi, always extremely penitent after misbehaving, remembered that her parents had married on Friday the thirteenth. Looking as sad as a Bassett hound, she said, "I'm their bad luck." When Ruth was told about it, her reaction was immediate and intense. "She is *not*," she said protectively. GiGi later wrote of her:

"My dream was to be like my mother. She's very gifted, intelligent, sweet, and mature. You have a lot to live up to family wise."

Ned came home from kindergarten and told his mother, "There's a boy at school what'n I don't like."

"Why don't you like him?" asked Ruth.

"Him's always pickin' on me," Ned replied.

"How does he pick on you?" asked Ruth with motherly concern.

"Everytime my knock his blocks down, him tells the teacher on me."

Ruth and the children were taking a walk down the asphalt road leading to their home. In one area the asphalt had a small bubble in it, and at Ruth's suggestion the children were trying to guess what was under it. After several guesses from the children, Bunny said, "It's a morning glory, and it's the glory comin' up."

Bunny, referring to a social gathering that was to be held at a future date, told me, "Refreshments will be served between four and five. I don't get any because I'm three."

8
The Trip

As a reward for being normal children, partly angelic and partly mischievous, the little Graham girls and one of Cliff Barrow's little girls were to be allowed to go on the train to meet Billy in New York when he came home from his crusades in Europe.

To begin with, the children were weak, due to a virus that had gone through the family like a prairie fire. As soon as one would get out of bed, another would take her place. The trundle bed under Ruth's bed was reserved for such a time as this; and to be sick meant all kinds of treats and concessions, so no one was in a hurry to get well. There was a special doll that could be played with only when a child was ill. If anyone stayed too long in the trundle bed, it was considered "unfair and cheatin'."

One little sufferer was battling a high fever and her stomach was as unsettled as the world map. Asked what she thought the matter was, she said, tossing, "I think it's probably 'pendix goin' round."

Because Ruth was still wobbly from the flu, I went on the trip to help with the children. The following is an account of the trip, parts of which have previously been published in *Christian Herald* in an article entitled "The Littlest Grahams."

The last question Ruth asked before boarding the train wasn't "Do we have the tickets?" but "Do we have their blankets?" The faded watery blue and pink blankets had followed them like shadows almost from the time they were born, and each child would have turned navy blue with cold before sleeping under the wrong one. Inevitably, the blankets picked up germs and dirt as they were trailed behind their owners. But as any mother knows, a little soil is preferable to washing them often and taking a chance on an electrical power failure which would put the dryer out of commission, resulting in wet blankets, thus a blanketless night. Most mothers tremble at the prospect of such a night and would rather face the so-called little men from Mars.

Ruth took along all types and colors of pills, ready for any sickness that might rear its ugly head, and the children's doctor-grandfather had prescribed a tiny pinch of Dramamine to assure that the children and their mother would get at least a few winks of sleep.

Since Ruth was really ill, I insisted on keeping all of the children in my compartment.

The first thing, the two older little Grahams had a slight altercation. The second born began pushing and pulling all the gadgets in view and explaining what they were. The older one, because of her seniority, took a dim view of her sister's superior knowledge and said in a prickly voice, "Miss Priss, just because you rode with your kindergarten class from Black Mountain to Old Fort (five miles) is no reason you know everything in the world there is to know about trains!"

The next thing was a trip to the diner. I had to almost sit on them until the diner opened—then they ran all the way like starving jackals. During the meal, there was no incident except that I had to eat most of the five dinners because the children had lost their appetites somewhere between the compartment and the diner. (Ruth has said that children would never stop eating if it weren't for meal time.)

On the way out of the diner, things began to pick up. One of the lynx-eyed children spotted a diner drinking beer. At least she thought it was beer, she said, as she passed his table a time or two to make sure. Then a doomsday mood enveloped her. She told me in a coast-to-coast whisper about her fears of a drunk man being on the train. Of course, the beer drinker heard her and tried to assume a detached air toward the beer, acting as though it had been left by a previous diner. But the little sleuth wasn't fooled.

Though I agreed with her views, she apparently thought my attitude toward drinking was too soft. Before I could stop her, she'd hurried to the headwaiter, pulled him down to her size, and told him about the evils of drink. Because he seemed thoughtful, impressed, and cooperative, she was willing to leave the beerhead in his care for the time being. But before she left the diner, she sent several dark looks in the beer guzzler's direction and then loudly expressed her views on drink all the way to the compartment. (According to most reliable reports these days, it seems that her views have turned out to be correct and that alcohol is the worst drug problem in the nation.)

She was also the mortal enemy of cigarettes and had a little ditty she recited with all the dramatics one would use in giving the Gettysburg Address: "Tobacco is a filthy weed, and from the devil doth proceed; it picks your pockets, burns your clothes, and makes a chimney of your nose." Her little brother, Franklin, gave the best definition of a lighted cigarette that I've ever heard. He called it "a little stoplight." (Cigarettes are a lot more dangerous now that they run in packs.)

When we reached the compartment, they again kept busy for a while getting familiar with everything. Then one of them suddenly said, "I'm hot." I passed my hand over the air conditioner and then over my brow when I realized that the air conditioner had gone on the blink and that the windows were sealed shut.

Then I sat back and waited to see if the Dramamine would collapse the children before the heat did. It had been no easy feat getting the small dosage down them. After much shuttling back and forth from hand to mouth to throat and back again, the dosage was finally in place.

They got out their "cootsases" and got ready for bed. They all had new nightclothes for the trip, so for a while they were kept busy modeling. Then one of them excitedly told me that some man had seen them in their bathrobes. I looked out of the window and saw a man probably two city blocks away getting in his crops and oblivious to the passing train—but the experience made them as jumpy as Mexican beans.

We had prayers while stopping several times to switch berths, get water, and bandage a mosquito bite that was "bleedin' blood."

For a few seconds they were quiet. Then little Carrie Nation sat up with a jerk and in excited tumbling words said, "I forgot to tell my mother about there bein' a drunk man on this train." Before I could get my wits about me,

she'd plummeted to the floor and opened the compartment door. I told her that her mother could take care of
herself. She looked at me in disbelief and said, "Do you
think I would let my sick mother stay on this train
without knowing there was a drunk man on it?" With
that, she hurried away to alert her mother or anyone she
happened to meet. In about fifteen minutes, she was
back, but she didn't mention the beer drinker again. The
next day her mother told me she hadn't mentioned it to
her when she came to her compartment.

It was a night to remember. There were no icy blasts
from the air conditioner. A line began to form at the
water cooler—and I knew that these mountain-suckled
children would put up a fierce resistance to their first real
attack of hot weather. For a while they lapped water, then
climbed back into their berths. But they didn't stay there.
At first, the one in the upper berth used a ladder to get
down—then later ignored it and swung to the floor,
Tarzan style. They pried each other from the water cooler.
Then realizing they couldn't store water like camels, they
began an endless procession of filling cups, most of which
was sloshed out by the lurching train or a lurching child.

Finally, a child in the lower berth made the mistake of
saying she wasn't hot. The agonizing little blister in the
upper berth retorted, "Of course you aren't hot. You're
down there in a cool little room and I'm up here in this
dark little closet, burning up." So there was a quick
shuffling of children. It didn't help. She began to drink
water till she was waterlogged. Then she put on a notable
performance, moaning and thrashing around in despair.
She clutched her throat and said, "I'm dying"—then lay
motionless until she saw that her dramatics were having
no effect on anyone. She leaped up and turned on the

light, bringing everyone back into the picture. She suddenly spotted a tiny wall fan which, strangely enough, no one had seen. Turning it on and putting herself in front of it, she exulted, "Hasn't this been a wonderful trip! I can't wait till we plan another one, can you?" And she went quietly off to sleep.

I didn't need a crystal ball to tell me there were other crises just around the corner. Sleep was catching up with me when the youngest little girl pitched out of the lower berth. I put her back and brushed what she called "ants" off her sheet—crackers they'd eaten after turning down a Duncan Hines special in the dining car.

The train began an endless back-and-forth movement, starting, stopping, jerking forward, then backward— switching cars. The three-year-old began to scream. The only things she could compare the train motion with were the times the family jeep had gotten stuck in a mudhole on the mountain and was plunging back and forth in an attempt to get out. She sobbed hysterically, "This train is stuckt." I explained what was going on, but it didn't satisfy her. She began to wail melodramatically, "I'll never see my daddy again!" More explanations, but to no avail. She sobbed, "I still won't see him again; his boat will drowned." Finally, after exhausting explanations, she went off to sleep.

I was drifting off to sleep when there was a loud pounding on the door. It was the porter saying that the air conditioner had broken down and we were being transferred to another car.

When we finally got to New York, all of us and the suitcases were shoehorned and dovetailed into a taxi and we were on our way to the hotel. It wasn't as peaceful a ride as you might think. The children were scandalized to find out that anyone would charge another person to ride in his car and they let the driver know it—not by out-and-out comments, which would have been rude, but by loud whispers and fierce pantomime in full view of the driver's mirror. They watched the meter like a cat watches a rat and as the price spiraled, they were hardly on speaking terms with the embattled driver.

Central Park came into view and the crude manners of the taxi driver were forgotten. Then these children who had been stared at all their lives now had the opportunity to stare at the animals in Central Park.

In the hotel room they were exuberant—not doing any damage but having noisy fun, so much so that the housekeeper stuck her head in and asked, "Is anything the matter?" I said, "No, nothing," then added lamely, "Nothing unusual." They all went to Coney Island that night. I stayed at the hotel, feeling Coney Island would be anticlimatic.

Before they were to go on the *Queen Mary* (which Ruth said they regarded as their private yacht) she gathered them around her to have a prayer that they would be kind to the reporters (and I felt sure she was praying that the reporters would also be kind to them).

I had in mind writing cards to friends with the words, "Having a good time!" But the way I finally wrote it was: "Having a time!"

9

Discipline

All the Graham children were "up and at 'om" children and were reared with prayer and a paddle, as were their parents.

Ruth's mother said, laughing, "I used to start out spanking Ruth for one thing and end up spanking her for five or six."

Billy's mother said that one day she spanked "Billy Frank" so hard that she was ashamed of herself and followed him to school to give him a quarter. Reminiscing, with the clucking sounds of a mother, she added, "If I had it to do over again, I don't think I would have spanked him so often."

"And perhaps deprived the world of a Billy Graham?" a listener asked. Backtracking a little, she assured the questioner that she would have continued to follow the biblical instructions on child rearing.

Ruth has said many times that she'll put the Book of Proverbs in the Bible up against any book on child rearing ever written.

A certain platform speaker was telling her audience that she had it on high authority that you should never spank a child. When asked to name her authority, she named a well-known psychiatrist. Billy and Ruth would have named a much higher authority who disagreed with hers—God.

Parents have often been told, "Spare the rod and spoil the child." (On one occasion, when Ruth's little brother was due for a spanking, his mother, in explanation, quoted that. Her little son said, "Then why don't you do what it says? You never spare the rod and you don't spoil me."

Both Billy and Ruth felt that a child's Creator should know best how he should be reared, so they listened to what he had to say. In brief communiqués from heaven, God says: "The rod and reproof give wisdom: but a child left to himself bringeth his mother to shame" (Prov. 29:15).

"Chasten thy son while there is hope, and let not thy soul spare for his crying" (Prov. 19:18).

"Foolishness is bound in the heart of a child; but the rod of correction shall drive it far from him" (Prov. 22:15).

God isn't speaking here to parents who are bombed out on alcohol or other drugs nor to child abusers, both of whom have at least temporarily abdicated their rights as parents. The Bible warns, "Parents, provoke not your children to wrath, but bring them up in the nurture and admonition of the Lord" (Eph. 6:4).

Most normal people seem glad that the Graham children were normal, as were their parents.

At one time when one of the little Graham children was misbehaving, someone foolishly asked Ruth how it was possible that a child of Billy Graham could fail to behave. Ruth answered, "They have me in them, too." Ruth has said several times, "Rosa and I fought like cats and dogs."

Relatives of Billy have said that he had a perfectly normal childhood—teasing his sisters and cousins, pulling their hair, hating to go to the Presbyterian church with his parents, and calling his mother's devotion "hogwash." He had many a whipping with his dad's belt and even more switchings with his mother's hickory switch.

Billy and Ruth don't agree with the woman who said, "I'd see my children's faults if they had any," but they also realize that children of people in the limelight sometimes have problems not experienced by other children. Ruth said that one day a teacher introduced one of their little girls on her first day at school as the daughter of Billy Graham and a child spoke up, "Then I hate her."

Ruth has had to be the disciplinarian in the family due to Billy's absences—but even when he's home, he's admitted publicly, "I'd rather plow a field than take them all on at once."

Ruth often used the humor she's famous for in dealing with the children. One day I heard her say to a misbehaving child, "If you don't behave, I won't let you have your tonsils out."

If she criticized a child, she'd often precede or follow the criticism with praise or encouragement. Ruth remembers an incident told her by an older friend who had been a kindergarten teacher. On this particular day, one of the little boys in the class had almost made a zombie out of her. Finally, unable to cope with him any longer, she blurted out, "Just remember, I've made a list of all your bad points." The child left the room, dejected and despondent. After a while there was a faint knock on her door. It was the little boy; he asked, "Did you remember to make a list of my good points, too?" She was ashamed. Ruth has little reason to be ashamed.

When Ruth was asked about her successes or failures as a mother, she said, "You'd best ask my children." Her children have nothing but the highest praise for her. GiGi said, "I want to be just like her." GiGi, mother of six, freely admits that she sometimes yells at her children. When she asked her mother why she'd never yelled at them when they were little, Ruth said, "I did. I prayed you wouldn't remember." (If she yelled, she must have yelled softly because I haven't found anyone who ever heard her.)

Franklin, the older son, admits that there were times when he'd come in at four in the morning and her light would always be on—yet the next morning she'd always be sparkly and cheerful and would never let on about the loss of sleep—or, more to the point, the concern she'd experienced until he was in. (Those who know her habits know that much of the waiting was spent in prayer. She's often said, "Drop to your knees and grow there.")

The only criticism her children could offer was that she took the burdens of other people on herself, yet refused to burden them with hers. There was the time she went to the hospital, thinking she might have heart trouble. She didn't mention it to them. Her attitude was and is, "I have the Lord. Who else do I need?"

As some of the antics of the Graham children are chronicled here, it's well for readers to remember the pertinent words confessed to me by a missionary on furlough. He said, "The martyrs on the mission field are those of us who have to live with the saints." Also, it's important to wait until you've heard the words, "Now you know the rest of the story," before you form a judgment.

GiGi is the eldest Graham child. Ruth wrote in GiGi's book, *Thank You, Lord, for My Home,* "Everybody should have a GiGi to raise. She was a terror, believe it or not." Then she gives a hilarious account of one of GiGi's escapades when she was a little girl. "I remember coming home—I don't know where I'd been—and our maid met us at the door and said, "Mrs. Graham, I don't know what's getting into the children, but they went up to the neighbor's house and sassed her."

"Well, now, this comes under moral issues, so I went upstairs with the little shoe tree and GiGi saw me coming. She was always the spokesman for the group; she was the one that usually thought up the mischief and got the others to carry it out. Basically, she is a shy individual, but, boy, can she think up things. She heard me coming, so she started in before I hit the door.

"She said, 'Mother, you can't blame me. It wasn't our fault. It was the devil! He's the one that got into us and he's the one that made us do it! Mother, you just can't blame us!'

"And I said, 'I realize, GiGi, that it was the devil. And what I'm going to do is beat him out,' which I proceeded to do. I had to leave again for about two hours and when I came back, our maid said, 'Mrs. Graham, I don't know what happened, but they've done the same thing over again.'

"Well, this time I shot up those steps, two at a time, and GiGi heard me coming and started in.

"'Mamma, you can't blame me. You know it was the devil that got into us.' All of a sudden she saw my face and said, 'But Mother, as soon as he saw you coming, he left.'

"So you see what I mean; Everybody ought to have at least one GiGi."[1] (Even the baby took his cue from GiGi and tried to palm off his misbehavior on the devil. He'd say, his eyes bright with innocence, "Debbil dood it.")

One day young GiGi burst into the kitchen, followed as usual by her two smaller sisters (her "back up troops" and "hit men"). She was almost incoherent, gesturing with her hands and talking with the speed of a tobacco auctioneer. Her eyes were bulging with shocked disbelief as she shouted to her mother that a woman down the road had chased them out of her yard with a broom.

"Was she riding it?" Ruth asked indifferently, hardly glancing up from her work at the sink. Ruth refused to "harpoon anchovies" or make mountains out of molehills.

GiGi, still loudly airing her outrage but somewhat deflated by her mother's mild reaction to her mind-blowing news, whipped around on her heels and swept off stage with the sisters in tow. (The three sisters, all grown with families of their own, have a deep love for each other which is strongly rooted in family ties. One sister told me that her sisters were still her best friends, echoing the feelings of the other two.)

Ruth told that on one car trip, GiGi had kept the car occupants in a churning uproar for miles, continuing in the full hearing of the gas station attendant when they drove in for gas. Then, as always, when she'd misbehaved, she experienced guilt feelings and an urge to "walk the sawdust trail" in remorse; but she still wasn't up to admitting her guilt outright. So she suddenly donned a halo, sprouted wings, turned her back on her recent past, and asked sweetly, "Why can't everybody sing hymns and be happy?" Then she hurriedly fished out a salvation tract, intending to give it to the attendant.

Ruth, knowing that the attendant had been a spectator

to the exhibition she'd put on, said sternly, "If you give him that tract, I'll clobber you!"

GiGi has never been lukewarm in any of her undertakings, which is just as well since the Bible says that if anyone is lukewarm in his works, God will spew him out of his mouth (Rev. 3:16).

A friend noted that GiGi, even during the process of rearing six active children, was calmer than she was as a child. Another friend laughed and said, "She's not calmer. She's just tired."

A friend of GiGi's mother, knowing that young GiGi had started taking piano lessons the week before, asked GiGi how she was getting along with her piano. GiGi informed her archly, "I've already learned piano." And knowing GiGi, who could doubt it?

After GiGi's first book was published, one of her older friends wrote her, "I once voted you the baby most likely to be left on somebody's doorstep"—then she poured on the praise for the wonderful mother GiGi had turned out to be. She also recalled GiGi's love for Christ when she was a child. In particular she remembered GiGi saying, "You can trust the Man who died for you." A person who knows GiGi better than most says of her, "She's one of the few people I trust" and continued, "She's one of the most deeply spiritual people I know."

When one of GiGi's older friends, who had watched GiGi grow up, told her husband, "As a child, your wife was a humdinger," he grinned and said, "She still is." And those who know, appreciate, and love GiGi are more than satisfied with his verdict.

GiGi, like her two sisters, is a lovely-looking, slim mother, though a friend remembers seeing her, as a child, look into the mirror and complain bitterly that she looked "just like a witch." GiGi is married to a man she met in Switzerland when she was a teenager. She has written two books and appears on Christian and other talk shows. She and her husband were concerned that their six children be listed in the Lamb's Book of Life rather than a social register, so they moved bag and baggage to Florida, where her husband practices as a Christian psychologist. The family attends a church where the Bible is accepted and taught as the infallible Word of God, and the children are entered in the Christian school connected with the church.

Anne, the second lovely-looking daughter, is married to a dentist in North Carolina who played on the University of North Carolina basketball team the first year it was the top team in the nation. It won again in 1982. She met him at one of the Christian Athlete Conferences; they have three children. Before her marriage, Anne was the horsewoman of the family and, for a time, a model.

One day Ruth heard the youngest little girl crying. She hurried to the kitchen and found Anne, a little older, slapping her sister first on one cheek and then the other. She explained to her mother, "I'm teaching her the Bible—to turn her cheek when she gets slapped."

Anne is still teaching the Bible—to a class of 500 with 240 on the waiting list. She was given permission to start the class as her Junior League project; but, finding she has to get up around five o'clock to study as well as taking care of her family responsibilities, she resigned her membership in the Junior League. Feeling that indiscriminate viewing of TV poses dangers for their three children, Anne says they're not allowed to even turn it on without either her permission or their dad's.

Bunny is the youngest Graham girl. Ruth called her

Bunny because she said that at birth, she looked like one. When she was small she habitually got an "A" in deportment at home and because of it, didn't get spankings by her mother. Then she suddenly did an about-face and became, by comparison, almost incorrigible—driving her mother up the wall with her new life-style. Finally, her mother was forced to give her a good spanking. Instead of yelling like she was being pistol-whipped (like some children, gently spanked, do for effect), Bunny rushed into the yard and bragged about the spanking. She said happily, "Mamma loves me. She spanked me." Many psychiatrists agree with the Bible that a child needs the security that discipline gives.

One day little Bunny fell victim to the baby, who spent his time either biting people or planning to. She wailed plaintively to her mother, "Can't we put him in a cage? I'll be an old, beat-up woman before I'm half grown and nobody will marry me." Feeling a wave of remorse the baby said, "Oh, I'll marry you, Bunny." Bunny continued, "I need to get away. I've got too much family."

Though there were no signs around, "Beware of the baby," the children would warn visitors who might become victims, "Pull his hair; it's the only way." And if a visitor showed any queasiness about doing it, they'd put on a live demonstration as to how it was to be done. When the baby started to cry, in a rush of tenderness, they were hugging and kissing him and giving him his rightful place in the family as king of all he surveyed.

Bunny was written up in *Good Housekeeping* as a beauty, with porcelain skin, blonde hair, and blue eyes like her daddy. The article mentioned her "swinging clothes," which her mother insisted were just stylish. (Older friends remember that as a little girl she changed outfits every hour on the hour.) She was known at an early age as being a meticulous housekeeper; her sisters insisted that she even dusted the flowers in the windowboxes and yard.

Bunny speaks of herself as "pugnaciously opinionated," which her mother says is merely "strong-willed."

Bunny is married to a man who films Billy's crusades as well as raising a rare breed of horse. They have three children. Many years ago, Bunny was already into her third Bible. She's written a book for children and also appears on Christian talk shows. I heard her say on a television program that the most important thing in her life was to know that her children loved the Lord.

Ned is the youngest of the Graham children. As a child he had an angelic-looking face which he now partially covers with a mustache.

He's had quite a few interests: for a while, he dipped into the field of photography. Later he studied fish and their habits. He spent a year studying in England. Later he became greatly interested in sports—karate was on the list—then swimming, in which he excelled to the point of having his coach suggest that he train for the Olympics. But in Ned's own words, "There's no way I'm going to stay in the water eight hours a day."

Next came the dangerous sport of rock climbing—his favorite. Knowing its dangers, Ruth insisted that he buy the best equipment available, saying, "It's cheaper than a coffin." However, two important happenings came out of his rock-climbing experiences. He had a serious fall which resulted in a badly crushed elbow. When he went to Mayo's in connection with the treatment of his elbow, he met the nurse who was to later become his wife.

At one time, Ned had wanted to drop out of college for a year in order to decide the direction his life would take. Billy and Ruth acquiesced, provided he'd agree to support himself that year. He got a job in a store which sold sports equipment. But Ruth later remarked that she didn't know how long she could afford for him to be a salesman, saying that once when he'd failed to meet his sales quota, he'd called her and asked her to come to the store and buy something to boost his ratings.

Ned, like his mother, had a good bit of the practical joker in him. As a child, he almost gave a friend of his mother's cardiac arrest when he threatened to pull off her wig in church. At first she confidently dismissed his threat, saying to herself, "He *wouldn't*! Then, recalling his penchant for jokes, she asked herself, "He *wouldn't?*" (So with Ned as a big question mark, maybe the best approach would be to stay home and listen to the service on the radio.)

But Ned wasn't all prankster. Early in life he made choices that hinted at what kind of man he was destined to become. On one of his childhood birthdays, an older friend gave him money, telling him to select something that he particularly wanted for himself. Instead, he insisted on giving the money to a friend who was trying to better the condition of people who had leprosy. (The more acceptable name is Hansen's Disease.)

On another occasion, as an older friend remembers, Ned, probably aged nine or ten, had gone to bed. He heard her playing the piano in the living room and called down to ask her to play "Amazing Grace" (which was a hymn popular with Christians long before it became a top hit recording in the music world). She said that she had to play it for him probably ten times before he finally dropped off to sleep.

Although all of the children love their home and make a beeline for it every chance they get, Ned seemed to be the most sentimental about it. Being six years younger than Franklin, who was the second youngest, Ned was home with Ruth long after the others were married or off at college. Trying to staunch the flow of invitations to speak, Ruth wrote regarding Ned's being the only child at home, "Now that his brothers and sisters are all gone, he needs me more than ever."

Ned speaks of the great times he and his mother shared, rattling around in the nearly empty home. Because Billy was gone so much of the time, Ned gives his mother credit for an unusual interest in him and all his projects.

Before his marriage, he went home for a last visit with Ruth; he said it seemed like the natural thing to do.

Before leaving, he took a prolonged tour through the home where he'd experienced so much love and warmth. After drinking in the details of each and every loved object which had been a part of him since boyhood, he was experiencing something akin to a hallowed moment as he said to his mother, with an ache as big as the whole outdoors, "It'll never be the same again!"

No one understood his thoughts better than his mother, who had drunk deeply of the dregs of cutting ties that had bound her to people and places she loved as well as experiencing the "vacant chairs" thrust into her life.

Later, Ruth recalled to a friend Ned's remark that "It'll never be the same again." Ruth said stoically to ease the hurt, "That's as it should be"—then, accepting God's plan of one phase of life following another, she said matter-of-factly, "I'm tired of diapers."

One Sunday, I sat near Billy and Franklin in church when Franklin was a very small boy. When the offering plate was passed, Franklin confidently dipped in, putting in a coin and taking one out. Billy looked like he'd go into shock. He grabbed his little son's hand and held it like it was in a vise. Franklin was bewildered and indignant. "I'm makin' *change*," he told his dad. (Perhaps Billy didn't think that putting in a nickel and taking out a quarter was acceptable. Parents can be so baffling.)

Ruth had a similar experience with him. She remembers: "Music played quietly as the offering plate reached our row. Out of the corner of my eye, I saw Franklin dip his hand into the offering. Quick as a flash, I grabbed the five-year-old-fist. Looking up, an aggrieved expression on his little-boy face, he exclaimed loud enough for all about us to hear, 'I was only hiding my penny under his dollar.'

"Aware of the suppressed smiles around us, I could only think of how often I had been guilty of the same thing: trying to hide my penny under someone else's dollar."[2]

Another time, when Franklin was about the same age, Ruth was horrified to hear him on a rampage in the yard, yelling and using the words H---, D---, and other descriptive ones. She rushed out of the house, devastated, wondering if she'd have to ship him off to a reform school. Seeing her coming and noting the incredulous look on his mother's face, Franklin said, perplexed, "I'm *preaching*!" As well as he could remember it, he was giving a replay of the sermon he'd heard Billy preach on his radio program, *The Hour of Decision*.

About this time, he also began to say "Shut up" to his

sisters or anyone in hearing distance. In order to nip the habit in the bud, Ruth laid down the law that he'd be punished whenever he did it. One day he forgot and yelled, "Shut up." Seeing Ruth bearing down on him, his voice quickly mellowed to a creamy liquid cadence as he added, hopefully, "My dear."

On one occasion, Franklin was pestering a teenage visitor in the home. No matter how hard the youth tried, he couldn't get three-year-old Franklin off his back. So he finally opened the door to the woodbox next to the fireplace, put Franklin in it, and shut the door. Franklin said, "I'll give you till I count ten to let me outa here." He started counting, "One, two, three"—then silence. The teenager said, "What's wrong in there, Franklin?" Little Franklin, subdued, answered, "I can't count any higher." (He and Lawrence Welk.)

One day, Ruth was advised that Franklin and his dog were lying dormant—stretched across the highway in their little town. Cars were backed up like a pileup on the California Freeway. Ruth says she jerked him up and switched his backsides all the way home.

A teenage friend of Ruth's was discussing with her the fact that a particular segment of the world's population believed that every person is born with a divine nature. He told Ruth, laughing, "They didn't know Franklin at six."

One day Ruth told Franklin to pick up the watermelon rinds he'd left on the porch and put them in the garbage can. He told her he didn't leave them. She knew he did and insisted that he admit it. He persisted in saying he didn't do it, so she finally told him they'd pray about it. After the Amen, Franklin still wouldn't admit to anything so Ruth said, "Well, *God* knows you did it." Franklin was thoughtful for a second and then said, "He doesn't *know*; he's just *guessing.*" The years have proved otherwise, and this once recalcitrant child is now a humble, dedicated witness to Christ's transforming power in a person's life.

Franklin is married to an exuberant girl he met at a Christian conference. They have three little boys. When Franklin was once asked by his mother what he planned to do with his life, he said, "I think I'll just sit around." He hasn't. He's president of an organization called Samaritan's Purse, which helps refugees, and is also president of a group called World Medical Missions, which Billy says he's built from scratch. He signs up Christian surgeons who are willing to volunteer for part-time service in different parts of the world. A requirement is that they be willing to give a Christian witness.

Probably no one, not even his parents, suspected that the body of this mischievous tot cloaked the man who would one day be brushed by the fire of the Holy Spirit and tapped on the shoulder by God for service. In any event, it's fairly certain that Franklin will one day stride to the lectern and, as his dad has done, preach the good news of salvation to anyone who will listen. And many *have* listened and have been impressed with the way God has dealt with him.

All this change took place silently. There were no voices, no strains of heavenly music, no pealing of bells, no rending of the heavens. Yet when Franklin made the statement that he wanted to spend time with his dad to help him in any possible way—if just to carry his bags or shine his shoes—those who have known Franklin from birth knew that a metamorphasis had taken place—that his once flinty resistance to Christ had been replaced by the humble acknowledgment that Christ was the one and only Lord of his life.

I suddenly remembered that many years ago I had been given a brief foretaste of what God had placed in the heart of this lovable four-year-old bundle of impish mischief riding beside me in the car as we drove down the mountain. The car suddenly slipped off the mountain road into a ditch. Surprised at seeing a worried expression on my face, the child said confidently, "My *Lord* will get you out."

As the scales fall from your eyes and you see the ways that God mysteriously works in the lives of people, you're overwhelmed by the wonder of it all.

In the lives of these five small and very human children, you were given only a hint of trailing clouds of glory. It's only now that you can appreciate the words, "Now you know the rest of the story." Embedded forever in your mind are the words of the Bible, "He which hath begun a good work in you will perform it until the day of Jesus Christ" (Phil. 1:6) and "The Lord will perfect that which concerneth me" (Ps. 138:8). We understand now why Jesus said of little children, "Suffer the little children to come unto me, and forbid them not: for of such is the kingdom of God" (Mark 10:14).

Notes

1. Taken from *Thank You, Lord, for My Home,* copyright © by GiGi Graham Tchividjian. Used by permission.
2. From *It's My Turn* by Ruth Bell Graham copyright © 1982 by Ruth Bell Graham. Published by Fleming H. Revell Company. Used by permission.

Billy reads *The Story of Jesus* to daughters Bunny (left), GiGi (standing), and Anne (kneeling). Used by permission of and copyright by Ruth Bell Graham.

Bunny, Anne, and GiGi (from left). Used by permission of and copyright by Ruth Bell Graham.

Left: GiGi. *Right:* Franklin. Used by permission of and copyright by Ruth Bell Graham.

Upper: Ned and Franklin (from left). *Lower:* Billy and Ned. Used by permission of and copyright by Ruth Bell Graham.

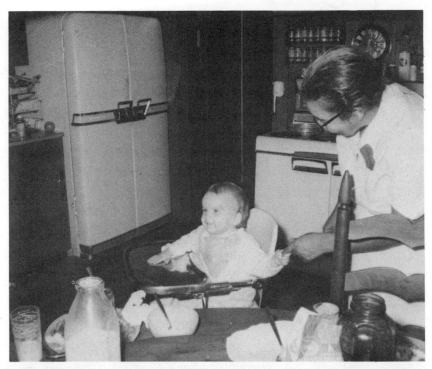

Ned and Bea Long. Used by permission of and copyright by Ruth Bell Graham.

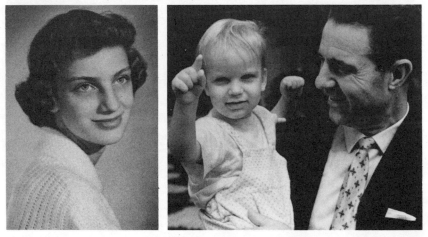

Left: Anne. *Right:* Ned and Lee Fisher. Used by permission of and copyright by Ruth Bell Graham.

Upper: Anne. *Lower:* Ned. Used by permission of and copyright by Ruth Bell Graham.

Left: Franklin, Ned, and Bunny (from left). *Upper:* Ruth and Anne. *Lower right:* Bunny. Used by permission of and copyright by Ruth Bell Graham.

Upper: Anne shares a special moment with Ruth on her wedding day. Used by permission of and copyright by Ruth Bell Graham. *Lower:* Billy, T. W. Wilson (left), and friends in Vietnam. Used by permission of and copyright by Betty Frist.

Clockwise: Ruth Bell Graham, Virginia (Mrs. Nelson) Bell, GiGi's daughter Birgette, Bunny, GiGi, and Betty Frist. Used by permission of and copyright by Ruth Bell Graham.

10
The Faith
of the Children

The Graham children knew the facts of life—eternal life. But Billy wanted to be sure they also knew the physical facts of life in a wholesome manner, so he suggested to Ruth that they raise animals on their property so the children could be properly instructed. Ruth, ever practical, said, "Why not just *tell* them and save ourselves all that trouble?"

The children and grandchildren have learned spiritual truths from many sources: Bible reading and prayer at family devotions, Sunday hymn sings, their own private devotions, Bible quizzes, games and Scripture memorization, attendance at a local conservative Presbyterian church, and, for some, attendance at Christian schools. From early childhood they've heard their dad's messages on the radio and televised crusades, as well as a daily diet of spiritual messages from great Christian leaders emanating from WFGW, the association radio station a few miles from their home.

All this is bound to have its effect on their thinking. Ruth, grinning, told that one little grandson who felt he'd had a little too much of it said, "Everybody's always talkin' about God up here." Ruth wisely warns that it's possible to try to cram too much too fast into a child—like trying to force too much too fast into a narrow-necked bottle. Ruth then told about this same grandchild who was present at a Christmas family gathering. After listening to the Bethlehem Christmas story read from the Bible by Billy, he was still being held back from opening his presents because one of his aunts wanted to record on film the family get-together. Finally he exploded, "Bethlehem was never *this* miserable."

Family devotion times were happy times, a secretary remembers—often with the children reading Scripture portions and leading in prayer (the prayers originating in their hearts instead of their using formal written prayers). Sometimes each child would select a verse from a little box of Bible verses called "Precious Promises."

When Billy was away, Ruth led the family devotions. Her prayers were always down to earth and practical— personal conversations with God, her Father, who was concerned with every tiny detail of their lives, as is promised in his Word, where we're told that he even knows the number of hairs on our heads, as well as noting the sparrow's fall.

God was made real to the children as Ruth prayed about their daddy and his work, Anne's cold, Franklin's studies, Bunny's concern over a sick pet, Ned's contemplated visit with a friend, and GiGi's interest in a current boyfriend.

The remarks that children inadvertently make are telltale signs of what is real to them. To Franklin, God was a living reality. Ruth's secretary wrote, "Franklin and I were sitting on the porch watching the lightning in the distance. When I asked him where the lightning came from, he explained that God made the lightning behind the clouds and then threw it like a ball across the skies. As the lightning began to subside, Franklin suggested that we continue watching the skies, for he *knew* it would start up again. 'How do you know?' I inquired. He answered, 'Because the Lord is over behind that cloud winding up.'"

Much of the children's lives were taken up with thoughts of Jesus and his love for them, so it was natural that they wanted to show their love for him. Ruth's secretary told that when Bunny was just a tot she wrote a song titled, "I have a little golden rocking chair for Jesus." The secretary said concerning the song, "At that age, one wouldn't expect the words to rhyme or the tune to be too melodious, but it contained so much love and sweetness that it probably sounded better than the Hallelujah Chorus to the Lord Jesus Christ."

The children were steeped in Scripture and seldom came face to face with a verse they didn't recognize. Anne, around twelve, had collected enough biblical knowledge to put many seminary graduates to shame. But one day I quoted an unfamiliar verse to her to show that a certain thing she professed to believe wasn't exactly in keeping with what the Bible said. I chuckled as Anne rushed to her mother and burst out, "Aunt Betty makes me so *mad*! She makes up anything she wants and says it's from the Bible." (I'd better *not* make up anything in view of the dire warnings in the Bible about adding to or taking away from the words of Scripture.)

When GiGi was a little girl, she threw a hand grenade into the conversation when she told her mother she wasn't saved because she couldn't find her name in the Bible. Ruth got up and took a piece of candy. Holding it out, she said, "Whoever wants it, take it." GiGi grabbed it, and Ruth said sternly, "Give it back! I didn't say you

could have it!" GiGi was indignant and shocked and said:
"You did too say I could have it! You said, Whoever wants
it take it!" You could almost see the wheels turning in her
head as the truth dawned on her. "Whosoever means *me*."
GiGi was convinced. "And whosoever will, let him take
the water of life freely" (Rev. 22:17).

"For God so loved the world, that he gave his only
begotten Son, that whosoever believeth in him should not
perish, but have everlasting life" (John 3:16). "Believeth"
means more than a historical belief. It means, as Billy
says, "Putting our entire weight on him." (The Bible says
that even the devils believed and trembled. They weren't
saved.)

Ruth's secretary wrote about one incident: "Dinner
conversation was always enthusiastic and delightful. One
evening, however, Ruth and Billy detected that such
might not be the case, for the children were having a
little argument as they arrived in the dining room. Billy
decided to nip it in the bud by announcing that if the
argument continued, the ones involved would be sent to
their room. As they sat down, they did so with the
argument totally unresolved. They apparently sensed
that if any of them said a word, the quarrel would begin
all over again.

"As dinner progressed, Ruth and Billy tried to get a
lively conversation going, but to no avail. The silence
continued. Finally Billy said, 'I commend you children.
This has been a quiet meal and I am proud of you for not
arguing' (or words to that effect). The silence continued
and he couldn't get a peep out of any of the little
Grahams. So he again said that he 'commended' them.
Still no response.

"Finally, he asked: 'GiGi, don't you have anything you
want to talk about?' 'Nope,' answered GiGi, 'I'm afraid I
might break the commendment.'" (I've never been able to

make up my mind as to whether GiGi was pulling her daddy's leg, since she was capable of it. One thing is sure: She knew the Ten Commandments, and she also knew they were written with the finger of God and not a ball-point pen.)

All of the children took their prayer time seriously. They learned early from Scripture that they were to "come boldly unto the throne of grace, that we may obtain mercy, and find grace to help in time of need" (Heb. 4:16).

Their parents taught them from Scripture that, "There is one God, and one mediator between God and men, the man Christ Jesus; who gave himself a ransom for all" (1 Tim. 2:5-6). "And if any man sin, we have an advocate with the Father, Jesus Christ the righteous" (1 John 2:1).

When Bunny was small, she took her prayer life in a particularly serious manner, so much so that one Sunday at church her face registered her concern—to the point that the anguished expression on her face caused her sister and brother in the pew to giggle. She learned early that real prayer is not just flicking a petition upward and letting it go at that; she found out that sincere prayer is real work and takes dedicated time.

An older friend, knowing the faith of small children, once asked Bunny to help her pray about a seriously ill relative. Little Bunny, knowing that it would take time from play and other things, exploded in exasperation, "Oh, *no*! Not *another* one to pray for!" But immediately, her conscience pricked her and she gladly took on the assignment.

Just before her wedding, Bunny admitted to having a nightmare that left her a little upset. She dreamed she was beautifully dressed in her wedding finery, gown, and veil, and that she'd walked down the aisle of the church and out again with not a single person seeing her because their heads were bowed in prayer the full time. (A friend felt and said that Jesus would have understood her concern since his very first miracle at Cana of Galilee, though it was to show God's glory, also saved a bride's family from embarrassment when the refreshments gave out.)

The Graham children pray because they know God answers prayer and that they're never put on "hold." However, they know there are certain requirements that they themselves must fulfill first, and nothing is in fine print. They know from the Bible, "If I regard iniquity in my heart, the Lord will not hear me" (Ps. 66:18). (Any known sin must be repented of and given up). They know from Scripture that "Without faith it is impossible to please him" (Heb. 11:6).

They know that any prayer must be according to God's will. "And this is the confidence that we have in him, that, if we ask anything according to his will, he heareth us: and if we know that he hear us, whatsoever we ask, we know that we have the petitions that we desired of him" (1 John 5:14). "In everything by prayer and supplication with thanksgiving let your requests be made known unto God" (Phil. 4:6). In James 4:3 they read, "Ye ask and receive not, because ye ask amiss, that ye may consume it upon your lusts."

If God's requirements are fulfilled, the children know that the Bible says, "[He] is able to do exceeding abundantly above all that we ask or think" (Eph. 3:20). Jesus said, "If ye abide in me, and my words abide in you, ye shall ask what ye will, and it shall be done unto you" (John 15:7) and "Hitherto have ye asked nothing in my name: ask, and ye shall receive, that your joy may be full" (John 16:24).

Many years ago a little boy named Bobby was greatly

impressed by the appeal of a visiting missionary in his church; but, being a poor child, he had no money to give when the offering plate was passed. So he took the plate out of the usher's hand, placed it in the church aisle, stood in the aisle, and said, "I give myself." He grew up to be the great Robert Moffatt, who accomplished monumental things for Christ.

Each of the Graham children has, at one time or another, said to Christ, "I give myself," with a promise to follow wherever he leads.

Dr. Ernest Gordon, a well-known minister and author, once told about his little son, who had come home from school one day and said that one of his classmates in the first grade had told him there wasn't any God. Interested, Dr. Gordon asked his son to tell him what he'd done about it. The child said, "I hit him and told him, There is *too* a God. My daddy *knows* him." The Graham children can say the same thing about their daddy.

11
Potpourri

"The time has come," the Walrus said,
"To talk of many things:
Of shoes—and ships—and sealing wax—
Of cabbages—and kings—"

—Lewis Carroll
Through the Looking-Glass

Cur-few

A friend was spending the night in the Graham home when Ruth was away. Before she left, Ruth insisted that the guest sleep in her room with one of the dogs at the foot of her bed.

Later, someone asked if the dog had kept her awake. She answered, "No, I kept *him* awake. I kept turning on the light to see if he was looking at me."

Their dogs' main distinguishing characteristic was that they considered automobile tires the staff of life. They ate so much rubber off the tires of visiting cars, you could have bounced them.

As soon as they'd pick up the sound of an approaching car, they were out with a whoosh on piston legs to do battle with its tires, and a person was lucky if he could get his car turned around before they made a shambles of its paint job.

Then came the chilling race down the mountain, the dogs with ears laid back—a scene reminiscent of pioneer days with Indians in hot pursuit of the stagecoach. The monsters would throw themselves in front of the front wheels while the driver tried desperately to keep from splitting them down the middle.

The dogs that the Grahams raised from pups struck terror to visitors' hearts—Heidi especially. If ever a dog was misnamed, she was. She was a St. Bernard from the famed kennels in Switzerland and was supposed to be loving and gentle, but she had the disposition of a wounded elk.

I think the main reason these pet dogs had such unpleasant personalities was due to the endless flow of visitors into the yard, some even throwing rocks at them, and some saying, "Nice doggie!" while reaching for a stick. A sign on an animal's cage at a zoo expressed it perfectly. "This animal is vicious. It defends itself when attacked."

Heidi looked on everyone as a Blue Plate Special, and on one occasion even tried to take off Billy's arm. Someone said, "If a body has legs hanging down from it, she'll go after them." One friend said, joking, "She didn't bite me as often as she did strangers. We had a game we played until the day she died. She'd pretend she wasn't going to bite me and I'd pretend I believed her."

The fact that a wisp of a girl walked up to her, patted her, and said, "Hi, Kitty" was no sign anyone else could do it and live to tell it.

Little children express their feelings better than grown-ups. One frightened child said of one dog, "He tasted me." Another terrified child, fearful that a dog intended biting her, pleadingly told him, "I'm not cooked."

Ruth's advice to visitors was usually, "Don't act afraid," but nobody was acting.

One friend remembers an experience she had when she was staying in the Graham home. Two of the children who were fed up with traveling in Europe decided to leave their parents and come home to stay with her. She tells it this way: "One evening after an early supper, the silence became deafening and I knew the children were up to some mischief.

"Just about that time I heard a shot far up the mountain and I immediately knew they had broken a hard and fast rule never to touch their daddy's gun. Terrified that they'd accidentally shoot themselves before I got to them, I ran screaming up the mountain, 'Put that gun down at once!' I could hear them laughing. Then I heard one of them yell, 'Sic her, Heidi.' I knew that if the dog caught up with me, there'd be nothing left of me but a grease spot. So I started running back toward the house, high heels collapsing, arms flailing, and dislodging pebbles and rocks as I ran—and wondering when I'd feel Heidi's hot breath on my neck. With a last spurt of energy, I grabbed the handle of the screen door, opened it, and threw myself inside just as Heidi hit it full force from the outside.

"That night the children divided their time between getting on their knees, apologizing, rolling on the floor, and howling with laughter. Because I was so thankful that both they and I were still alive, I laughed too."

Just looking at Belshazzar was enough to scare a person to death. Ruth tells of a little visiting dog in the backseat of a car who caught a glimpse of him. She said, descriptively, "She took one look at Belshazzar, passed out, and didn't come to till the car reached Asheville (eighteen miles away)."

It was once mistakenly thought that Belshazzar had cancer of the foot. A friend whose car wheel had accidentally run over his foot when he was chasing the car wrote Ruth to find out if she had caused it. Knowing that this friend would have welcomed seeing Belshazzar made into a rug, Ruth wrote: "No, you didn't cause Belshazzar's cancer. Better luck next try."

As children, Billy and Ruth both had dogs. Ruth had a dog that was so mean he had to be put to sleep. But it was said that the more the dog was hated, the more Ruth loved him.

It's remembered about Billy that before the school bus picked him up in the mornings, Billy (strictly for laughs) would ride around the neighborhood on his bike, followed by his collie and two goats—one black and one brown.

There was a succession of dogs of all descriptions at the Grahams's. A little boy summed up his gratitude to God for all kinds of dogs in a letter to him: "Dear God, I'm glad how you made dogs in all flavors."

Billy enjoys his dogs. When he's not home, they're not allowed in the house. But as soon as he arrives, they look at Ruth with haughty disdain and follow him inside— making the house double as a kennel.

Not only did the Graham children have dogs; there were other animals. Tiny Tim was a big Belgian roan mare that had been misnamed as a colt. There was a ram that I called the Grahams's "Battering Ram." He got a bad press when he butted Billy down the mountain, injuring his knee. There were cats in abundance— Mouldy (who looked it), Marmy (the color of marmalade), Almost ("almost white," Bunny said), and Tuxedo (with the correct markings).

Any animal was acceptable. Ruth was a little upset when a neighbor, who had found a baby skunk in her garbage can, turned it loose instead of giving it to the children. Ruth's secretary remembers Ruth nursing a hamster back to health. There were also birds, and Ruth would have loved having as a pet one of the little bear cubs on their property if she could have caught up with it.

Cooking and Dining

When the family gathers at the table for a meal, every head is bowed in grateful thanks before any food is touched.

Mealtime at the Grahams is an unforgettable experience; as a former guest remarked, "I'd rather be invited there than to the White House or Camp David."

It's no greasy-spoon flophouse type of eating place because Ruth is a super cook, often fixing exotic meals from the many countries that she's visited. But since her home was China for a good many years, a guest might be offered a delicious Chinese fare, complete with chopsticks. However, with Ruth presiding over the kitchen, it could be anything from octopus pudding to turnip greens and scrapple, which Ruth says Billy learned to eat as a child—out of his dog's dish. Mainly, the food is simple and wholesome.

Ruth admits that Billy eats so high on the hog when he's entertained away from home that sometimes he can hardly wait to get home, go to the pantry, open a can of beans, and eat them cold right out of the can. She says he likes plain food. However, a friend once heard Billy say, sighing, "Not hamburgers *again,* Ruth!"

The table in the combination family-breakfast room is an antique that came out of one of the cabins that the Grahams bought. It has a Lazy Susan in the center which spins almost continually as hands of all sizes reach out to take food off as it goes by. There are many near misses, and if it should suddenly brake to a stop, the food is likely to fan out all over the room. Commenting on this when he was small, Franklin said, "What this thing needs is a stoplight."

(One morning, one of the little grandchildren who usually held in check so much energy that he was ready to explode in all directions had, in the space of possibly an hour, vigorously spun the Lazy Susan, throwing things north, south, east, and west; burned his little sister's shoes in the fireplace; and made a start in painting his

Uncle Ned's room with gilt paint. But on the plus side, when he was thirteen, he was working on his own Bible commentary, refusing even to join his sister and brothers to watch selected television programs.)

All of the children taught themselves to cook and were allowed to try their hand in the kitchen when it wasn't occupied with meal preparation. One day young GiGi was cooking steak for company on the outside grill. The steak fell through the grill into the ashes and GiGi fished it out, rushed it to the sink, washed it with detergent, rinsed it, and put it back on the grill. One of the guests said, "Steak is steak, and nobody complained."

Ruth's secretary reminisced about some of the things that were etched in her memory while she lived in the home: "The harvest table in the dining room with the pot marks" (it was an antique which had originally served as a kitchen table); "the ping-pong table set up over the dining room table to accommodate the Thanksgiving meal; the dining room chair that had a habit of falling over as an unsuspecting guest started to get up; link sausages and fried apples for breakfast; the way Ned loved apple butter; the time he was found basting the chicken with three-in-one oil; the way Franklin loved 'spickets' (biscuits); company dinner with lamb roast, apples, rice and gravy, string beans, rolls, and Bea's apple pie; snow ice cream and maple sugar candy; Franklin, the little ole bacon snitcher, also sneaking a piece of dough when Bea was making biscuits, or sneaking behind her and tickling her in the ribs." Then there was the time that Franklin helped his mother spoon dressing into the turkey. When the bird was carved, everyone was fascinated as Dr. Bell spooned out the spoon with the dressing. Franklin had tucked it neatly away and forgotten it.

Little Franklin was usually very much in evidence. During the time he went through his "spitting" stage, he spit on a teenage friend who immediately spit back, embarrassing the mother of the teenager; but Ruth felt that Franklin had it coming to him in order to break him of the habit. Nevertheless, the teen's mother told him he had to call Ruth and apologize. She later heard him on the phone saying, "Ruth, Mama says I have to tell you I'm sorry I spit on Franklin, but I'm not." It was finally agreed between Ruth, the mother, and the teenager that he could fill his mouth with water and squirt it on Franklin in the event he spit on him again. That night Ruth called to invite him and his mother to dinner. When they got to the table, Ruth pointed to a gallon jug of water beside the teen's chair and said, "Your ammunition, Tommy."

One of Ruth's friends was happy when Ruth told her she could fix the deviled eggs for the Nixon luncheon, until Ruth pointed up her status as a cook by calling to her as she started home in her car, "Don't leave the shells in like you usually do." The friend said, "I didn't leave the shells in, but the eggs were pocked from being too fresh." Then she added, "But I don't think Mr. Nixon noticed them or me either."

A lot of people get in a lot of freeloading because Ruth is the soul of hospitality. And it's fun to eat there. A guest doesn't have to pick her way through rows of silver beside her plate, and now and then she might even spot a cup without a handle. (That reminds me of the mother of one of Ruth's acquaintances. She was looking around her daughter's house and said, with some irritation, "A houseful of museum pieces and not a cup with a handle.")

The simplicity of life at the Grahams coincides with the remark made by Bunny in answer to unfounded criticism: "We don't live in a mansion or have a yacht or a fleet of Cadillacs."

Race

After Billy refused to speak to a segregated audience in Birmingham, Alabama, Ruth wrote a friend, "We're expecting a cross-burning on our lawn at any time now." (During those hideous days, one person spoke of Birmingham as "Bombingham" in anger over the bombs that went off. She said she meant no reflection on the fine people who lived there and who also felt the same kind of anger against the extremists.)

Billy has no patience with racism and is magnificent in anger whenever it raises its ugly head.

I once heard a woman ask him, "Billy, you don't think God loves a little nigger boy as much as he loves my little grandson, do you?" Billy's steely blue eyes turned to oval ice cubes as he said with pile-driver force, withering the air around them, *"I certainly do!"* The conversation ended abruptly.

At one of Billy's crusades, the platform for the speakers was set up on a football field. One young man was so affected by the message he'd heard from Billy that he walked across the long field, sobbing. He had both hands raised, the forefinger on one pointing up to God and the fingers on the other hand making the V-for-Victory sign.

On reaching the platform, he continued to stand with his hands upraised and his head bowed in prayer. After a time, his arms began to tire and lower. A black minister on the platform saw what was happening, jumped off the platform, and hurried to stand behind the young man to hold up his faltering arms.

To the many Christians in the vast audience it was a

never-to-be-forgotten sight as they recalled a similar
scene from the Bible where Aaron and Hur held up the
hands of Moses as he prayed. When his hands were up,
the Israelites prevailed in battle; when they were
lowered, the enemy was victorious (Ex. 17:11-12).

In a lighter vein:

One of the Grahams's prized dogs was losing his sight
and was taken by Ruth and a friend to an animal hospital
in another state.

Ruth was dressed unostentatiously in an inconspicuous
dress and flats, while the friend was more or less gussied
up like "Stella Dallas."

Ruth has a gypsy cinnamon-colored skin—sort of a
"scorched" look from so much time spent in the sun. At
this particular time she'd overdone the time spent under
the sun's powerful rays and looked more charred than
scorched.

Word had leaked out that Mrs. Billy Graham was to be
there. When the two arrived, a secretary in the lobby
kept eyeing them and in a burst of uncontrollable enthusiasm rushed up to the friend and asked, "Are you Mrs.
Graham?" The friend said no and introduced her to Ruth,
later telling Ruth in high glee, "She thought it was Mrs.
Billy Graham and her black maid."

There was a black woman who was with the Grahams
from the time the children were little until she retired,
but she was far more than a maid. Ruth wrote about her,
"She's the joy of my life." She was second mother, confi-
dante, disciplinarian, and an indefatigable worker in her
church. When the family gathered to read the Bible and
knelt to pray each day, Bea Long would often lead in the
Bible reading and prayer. One of the little boys was heard
to say one morning, "Let Bea pray; she prays short and
good."

The children loved and respected her. I once saw the baby in her arms take her face between his two chubby hands and say in an outburst of love, "Bea, you're a good boy."

She rarely lost her cool, but one day she walked into the kitchen to see an almost professionally stuffed and dressed body on the floor with a knife (and the accompanying ketchup) in its back. Since it was dressed in the older Graham son's clothes, she said, "It put me to bed!"

A guest in the home, hoping to get a rise out of Billy and Ruth, said to another guest, "Bea is the best Christian up here." She fell flat on her face because Billy and Ruth heartily agreed.

Excerpts from Letters

From time to time, Ruth's letters written to friends through the years have surfaced. A sentence here and there or a fragment of a paragraph gives a quick glimpse into the everyday happenings connected with the children or some phase of their lives:

"Franklin is tough and wiry and as sweet as can be."

"Gorgeous George is beginning to call so I'll have to sign off for now." (Older readers will remember that Gorgeous George was a well-known wrestler for a short time.)

"Ned's the one I'm dying for you to see. He's little and fat and adorable and by summer, he'll be big and fat and maybe not so adorable."

From Switzerland: "We're having a great time with GiGi and Stephan and the family. They are so happy and have such a sweet little home." Concerning GiGi: "Isn't she terrific?"

"Anne is a lovely five feet seven and a half. Franklin is home from school with the bare possibility of a fractured liver. Ned is growing like a weed, and GiGi falls in and out of love with great enthusiasm. Bunny is still a character. As Franklin remarked one day, 'I wish I had Bunny's disposition. She approves of life.'"

"Anne is still on cloud 9—loves housekeeping, loves cooking, loves married life, loves living in Chapel Hill. Sorta sounds like they're happy. Bill is in Berlin. He plans to spend Christmas in Vietnam this year."

"It's time to walk down the mountain to meet the children."

"I'm sitting here and making some candied grapefruit peel and listening to Jill Corey sing *Robes of Calvary*."

"Ned is just over the mumps."

"I may not be the busiest woman in the world but I am undoubtedly the most disorganized. Bea was sick for three weeks beginning Christmas Eve. And Bill was home! You'd be amazed at how I got along. Then two weeks in Florida with GiGi and Anne and it was delightful. Now we're just getting over the flu. All four children had it at once. We really had a jolly hospital."

The Pool and Cabin

A friend tells about the early days when the children were small; she quotes GiGi, now a mother, who said, "I keep wishing for my own children the same experiences that all of us had together." One of their boy playmates, also married and living in a foreign country, said, "I hate the changes. I want it all to be exactly like it was then."

Ruth, commenting, said, "Wasn't it fun?"

Several days a week, Ruth would fill the car with their children and the mother and children of another family, plus, at times, other assorted children. They'd go antiquing through the mountain to find cabin furniture, go shopping in Asheville, or head for the pool to crisp the children in its icy water.

If they headed for Asheville, there was a tradition that had to be followed. When they reached the tunnel opening leading to the city, they'd all suck in their breath and hold it until they reached the other end. Death was preferable to failure. That was the only time they were quiet. Most of the time they were singing, often cafeteria style with each selecting his or her own tune and ignoring the rest, but often joining in joyful but murderous harmony when singing, "The Titanic." The song they loved to sing most was, "Do Lord, Oh, do Lord, Oh, do remember me."

On pool days Ruth would drive the jeep, and down the road it would come, clanking like a knight in armor. Happy children would fairly erupt from the houses when they'd hear the horn, which had a peculiar braying sound. Ruth would pat it and say, "It's sick." Then with the children hanging on to the sides, up the mountain they'd go, the jeep soaking up the jolts in the unpaved washboard road. One time Belshazzar and a dog about his size and disposition scared everybody out of their wits by getting in a fierce fight which neither won because they were evenly matched. After that, it was all noise and bluff because each was scared of the other, Ruth said.

In those days, the pool was a handmade affair—a mountain stream hemmed up with helter-skelter rocks which looked like they were held together with spray starch. You kept wondering if and when the whole thing would collapse and send children spewing all over the valley. (It's since been shored up and revamped by friends.) The pool had to be drained often because when furiously coiling black clouds loosed their torrents of water, the flash floods brought in tons of mud. Sometimes the stream below the pool was a thin scrawl of water, which hopefully could be dipped up with a cup. But when all this water was dumped from the skies, it became a monster water whip, curling and crashing its way down the mountain, looking as though it would take people and houses with it.

Due to the resulting deposited clay brought into the pool from the icy mountain stream, the pool was often the color and temperature of creamed, iced coffee. But as Ruth told an interviewer, it was a challenge with children, dogs, and bugs fighting to keep afloat and with each child trying to scuttle the one next to him.

Every few minutes a child would scream, "Help!—I'm drowning," and Ruth and a friend, as the rescue squad, would dive in only to find that the child was crying wolf. The children soon learned that such actions weren't to be permitted.

The children had frequent joyful times of banter— hurling so-called "insults" at each other. When the insulted one couldn't top the insult received, he or she would give an elegant shrug and wait for another opportunity. When one of the little girls would display, with all the fanfare of displaying the Hope Diamond, a little ragged stained tooth, she knew she could expect one of the boys to say something like, "Who wants to see your old beat-up fang?" But she also knew that he'd be willing to collect two black eyes in her defense. The children seemed fairly well matched, and between them was fashioned a bond of friendship which hopefully will last through all eternity.

Some years ago, one of the then-grown Graham girls laughingly said that she'd written a card to one of the pool playmates, also grown, and signed it, "An ignorant Fascist bigot," which, she said, still laughing, "is exactly what he called me when he left." It's evident that the fun still goes on.

Every few minutes a child, looking like a water rat and bluish purple with cold, would thrash her way out of the water to give Ruth wild-eyed briefings of what was going on in the pool. The one who happened to occupy the rubber float at the moment would ride by as though he or she owned a seat on the stock exchange and was as unpopular as someone who has just won a popularity contest.

One of the Graham girls recalled a pool tradition, that at summer's end one of their mother's friends would have to dive into the pool, fully clothed, even to high heels. But after the pool was remodeled and heated it became more or less a blah experience and was abandoned.

In those days Billy didn't often go into the pool, but a pair of faded swimming trunks hung on the limb of one of the trees most of the summer, mute evidence that once in a while in a burst of courage, he'd brave the icy flow and muddy water.

Sometimes the pool enthusiasts would spend the night in the little crude cabin. Ruth used to say that houses of that type ought to sell for more since they had no electrical fixtures and plumbing to get out of kilter, thus causing electric and plumbing bills. She also noted that a lot of money could be saved by leaving out the frills, like kitchens. Then she pointed to an old ragged newspaper picture of Bill hanging lopsided on a nail and said, "Wouldn't you think that picture of Bill would add about five dollars to the price?"

The children have grown up with almost savage speed. But as a friend recalls those slumber parties in the little cabin, with curtains hung on lengths of string, rather than rods, she says, "Nothing will ever erase the memory of those nights spent in the cabin. I can see the children's faces in the light from the flickering fireplace flames and oil lamps—intense as they thrilled and chilled to the ghost stories told in sepulchral tones. They snuggled closer together in shivery joy as the flames in the fireplace dropped lower and lower. Ruth could tell Bible stories so vividly that you might expect to shake the hand of David and shake your fist at Goliath when you met them around the next bend in the road.

"Prayers were finally said; sins were confessed and forgiven; and a jeepful of tired little children, confident of being wrapped in the love of God, were stored in a homogenized mass on loft pallets. Cuts and bruises and bickering were forgotten. Now and then a barely audible sigh was heard, and the children slept while walls of angels surrounded them."

Housekeeping

When one of the summer residents was due in Montreat, a thoughtful Ruth and her secretary went down to open her house and see that it looked its spit-and-polish best for her arrival. When the friend arrived, she opened the front door and at the threshold there was a carefully placed strip of paper cut from the cover of the *Good Housekeeping* Magazine. In the exact middle of the words "Good Housekeeping" lay a carefully arranged dead mouse, much the worse for wear.

After much prodding and argument pro and con, and at the friend's insistence, the culprits finally admitted that a dead mouse shows *good* housekeeping because rat poison had been put out—that a live mouse would have proved their point.

However, this same resident admits that when she's working on a project, housekeeping goes out of the window. She says that during such times, as a housekeeper she's a cross between Phyllis Diller and Ma Barker and never competes for the Good Housekeeping Award. Consequently, she says that the house looks like it's been stirred with a stick.

With this background, the teenage son of this woman got Ruth to fill out an application blank to help him land a "roughing it" type of summer job out West.

When Ruth came to the question "Can the applicant put up with pioneer conditions?" she had everyone laughing when she wrote in the space, "He always has."

When the children were little, Ruth used to insist that she was a "higgledy-piggedly housekeeper," though she wasn't. She just refused to make a fetish out of it if it meant neglecting the children. One day a reporter arrived for an interview before Ruth had time to get the house in shipshape condition. She explained the situation to him by quoting Proverbs 14:4: "Where no oxen are, the crib is clean." (With the children tracking in dirt on their shoes, someone wondered why Ruth didn't follow the Oriental custom adopted by her sister, Virginia; she and her husband are missionaries in Korea. When they were on furlough, a visitor to their home noticed that all of the family shoes were shed at the back door.)

On one occasion, a woman who was a housekeeping addict and who was to stay in the Graham home as housekeeper while Ruth was away on a trip, in order to emphasize Ruth's shoddy housekeeping, pointed to a spider web on the ceiling. When Ruth returned from the extended trip, she walked in the door, glanced at the ceiling, and said, "There's that same old spider web— only now it has a spider in it."

Sometimes Ruth would interrupt her housekeeping chores to take time out to help paint the roof or take a broken washing machine in hand to repair it. But even so, there was one picture window in their house that stayed so spotless that birds would hit it full force and knock themselves out cold—the end of the line for them.

Special events called for special cleaning. Ruth told how diligently she'd worked to get the house in perfect condition for the television camera crew filming the Billy Graham section of the famous Person-to-Person Series. The vacuum cleaner and dustcloth rarely ever came to a full stop. However, Ruth later recalled that she'd failed to take into account the powerful spotlights which mercilessly exposed every speck of dust that she'd missed. But since Ruth is adept at turning a bad situation into something helpful, she used the incident to illustrate the fact that God's powerful searchlight exposes the hidden ugliness of our lives. She tucks these happenings away in her mind and later expertly uses them to perk up a Bible lesson for young people or whoever happens along. (There's one place you can be sure no dust will ever be found—on Ruth's Bible.)

Ruth always insists that Billy is the neat one while

she's a more relaxed housekeeper. It's entirely possible that he's changed, but in the book *Billy Graham* the reader is told of one hostess who had Billy as a houseguest. She reported that his room was a shambles and that she'd picked up nearly a wastebasketful of items he'd left behind. Further mention was made of the fact that the top of Billy's desk was far from neat and that Ruth had never been able to cure him of the habit of using the top of the bathroom door as a towel rack.

A resident of Montreat remembers that when Billy was due home, one of his secretaries would rush to his study to get the stacks of books off the floor and back onto the shelves. She added, "The room looked like the public library on moving day."

One friend says, "I don't think Ruth gives a hoot about Billy using the top of the door as a towel rack, but now and then she's expressed concern over the fact that he sometimes speaks at crusades with his hair looking unkempt because of its length. She says he feels he doesn't have time to go to the barber shop. But she's threatened to put it in a ponytail if he doesn't."

Often Billy has more important things on his mind than what he wears; and in a hurry to get under way he'll sometimes throw together an assortment of wild colors such as red golf pants, blue T-shirt, yellow socks, and any color of cap handy. When Ruth mentioned that she was a little embarrassed over some of his outfits, a friend was reminded of what John D. Rockefeller said when he was told that he shouldn't keep appearing in public in wrinkled suits. He asked, "Who do I need to impress?"

Proving that Billy is interested in keeping things neat, some years back there were thousands of young people gathered for a meeting where Billy was the keynote speaker. At the close of several days of meetings, the head of the cleanup squad appeared on the platform to commend the young people for their neatness in their care of the grounds. He mentioned that in the entire area, only *one* piece of trash paper had been found. Billy quickly stepped to the lectern and asked in mock indignation, "Who dropped that piece of paper?"

When Mr. Nixon was leaving after his luncheon visit, Ruth called to him as he started down the driveway in the car, "Hurry back! It'll give me a chance to get the house clean."

Ignoring the fact that Ruth belittled herself as a housekeeper, she saw to it that there was a place for everything with everything in its place—unless, of course, you're going to count turtles in the bathtub or, now and then, dead crawfish on the windowsill over the sink.

Education

Both Billy and Ruth graduated from Wheaton College, which is known for its academic excellence; and both are avid readers of the books that fill almost every conceivable niche in their home. Billy is a speed reader. One observer noted with a straight face, "Billy can read an entire page while that little dot is going out on TV."

Some critics have questioned Billy's qualifications as a minister since he didn't have a formal seminary education, but his fans know he studied at the feet of the Holy Spirit himself.

Billy once insisted that no one had ever called him a great preacher. He maintains that there are thousands of ministers who are better preachers than he is. He's also said that he's no intellectual, claiming that the Bible has been his Harvard and Yale.

But listen to the words of the *Saturday Evening Post* in its spring issue of 1972 as it plows its words into the reader's mind:

"Make no mistake about it. This is no hillbilly boy from the North Carolina backwoods who suddenly took to religion but when he got the call, he got it to stay and has been following a simple creed ever since.

"This 51 year old man is a student and an intellectual. His study is crammed with religious books of all the ages, thousands of them—Bible concordances, the sermons of the great preachers of Europe and America, the philosophies of the world.

"His office complex down the valley has a library of even greater depth, perhaps 10,000 volumes covering every nuance and fact concerning the history of the world."

Among other things the article says, "The great and the simple seem to be drawn to Billy Graham. Winston Churchill, a man no one has ever accused of being lacking in intellect, said to Billy, 'I do not see much hope for the future unless it is the hope you are talking about, young man. We must have a return to God.'" The article made it clear that Billy also appealed to the hippie type who often came to jeer but stayed to pray.[1]

Billy and Ruth aren't aware of the source of my information, but some years ago I found out that the late Werner von Braun, the brilliant scientist who was called the Father of Space, kept Billy's book *Peace with God* on his bookshelf next to his Bible.

No one would deny that formal education has its rightful place on the world scene. But even an incredibly keen mind such as that of von Braun recognized the fact that though the Scriptures speak of the Apostles as "unlearned and ignorant men" (Acts 4:13), they also turned the world upside down, as was admitted by their critics. Noah Webster said that "Education is useless without the Bible." In 2 Timothy 3:7 we read, "Ever learning, and never able to come to the knowledge of the truth." In Matthew 11:25 Christ himself said, "Thou hast hid these things from the wise and prudent, and hast revealed them unto babes," and in 1 Corinthians 1:27 we read, "God hath chosen the foolish things of the world to confound the wise." And Jesus himself didn't mince matters in calling people fools who didn't believe everything the prophets said. He said, "O fools, and slow of heart to believe all that the prophets have spoken" (Luke 24:25).

A Phi Beta Kappa key is rightly looked on as a worthy and useful possession—yet it's a key that won't open heaven's gate. Someone has said that to educate a cannibal without accompanying the education with moral instruction amounts to teaching the cannibal to eat his victim with a knife and fork.

Ruth once remarked that some might look on it as heresy, but that she had talked with Ph.D.s who had bored her to death and to high school dropouts who fascinated her. Ruth has always been greedy for knowledge and is the direct descendant of a very unusual man who, when he fell from his horse one day, acquired a bruise on his head which kept him from speaking in English. But he continued to speak fluently in Latin and Greek.

Ruth told her daughters (all of them married early), "Keep reading and you'll be educated."

Some time ago, a letter Ruth had written to a friend

years ago came to light. She wrote, "I am reveling in good books (the Bible, of course)." Then naming several authors, she continued, "Here's a gem from McDonald—'It's only in Him that the soul has room' and 'Oh, the folly of the mind that will explain God before obeying Him.' And don't you love this from Jeremy Taylor, 'He threatens terrible things if we will not be happy.' Then she quotes an old Russian proverb, 'It's not the ocean that drains but the puddle.' Enough quotes. But they give me something to think about while sun bathing (plus memorizing Scripture verses—the greatest source of refreshment I know").

On the lighter side, Ruth was a little concerned that their older son was taking longer to graduate from college than she felt he should (though he was gathering information which has proved invaluable to him in his present work). After he finally graduated, Ruth informed him that one of his cousins had that very day graduated "with honors." Her son said, grinning, "I graduated with relief." (The Montreat Anderson College newspaper said later that he also graduated with honors.)

Included in a person's education is penmanship. Ruth's handwriting is as unusual as she is. A friend commented, "I'd recognize it if I saw it on a scrap of paper in the Sahara Desert. It's a beautiful script; but if a person isn't familiar with it, he might end up with his eyes crossed after trying to read one of her letters."

One friend tells that her husband called her from his office and said, "There's a letter here for you from Ruth. I'd read it to you over the phone, but I don't have time for a headache."

One afternoon several guests were in the Graham living room talking with a handwriting expert who had lectured in the area. Ruth suddenly left the room and brought back a treasured letter for the expert to analyze. The thrilled listeners heard her analyze the handwriting of a famous minister of another era, John Wesley.

The conversation about handwriting started a train of thought in at least one listener's mind—God's handwriting on the wall of Belshazzar's palace and its momentous prophecy which was accurately interpreted by God's own handwriting expert, Daniel (Dan. 5). Though critics have scoffed at the biblical account, clay tablets have been found that attest to the Bible's accuracy.

Dr. Melvin Grove Kyle, internationally famous archeologist, has said that no discovery in excavations has invalidated a single statement of the Bible. On the contrary, the discoveries have remarkably confirmed the Scriptures.

William Albright has said, "In general sweep and factual detail" the Scriptures have been found to be accurate "in a way not dreamed possible forty years ago."

Note

1. Reprinted with permission from The Saturday Evening Post Company, copyright © 1972.

The Hired Men

A certain factory owner was asked, "How many people work here?" He replied, "About half."

Ruth said of a particular hired man, "I pay him to talk, not work."

One hired man at the Graham house had little or no respect for rulers of nations, and in particular one he called "Joe Stallion."

Nor was he shy about voicing his political observations. He was to be in charge of the guest list when a prominent Republican was being entertained at lunch. One of Ruth's friends tried to explain the procedure to him, but either he didn't understand or pretended he didn't. Finally giving up on him, she said, "If they're Christian and Republican, let them in." He looked her straight in the eye and said coldly, "You know as well as I do that they can't be both." (Billy says he's a Democrat but votes independently—which made him practically a Benedict Arnold to the hired man.) With that in mind, the hired man told one of the Graham daughters who had shaken hands with the Republican visitor, "Well, it won't hurt you none if you'll hurry and wash your hands in Lysol."

When he heard that royalty dressed simply for lunch rather than wearing jewels, robes, and crowns to the table, he was shocked, feeling that people who were in the catbird seat ought to act like it. He told Ruth, "Now you looky here. I'd have said to 'em, 'If you ever expect *me* to visit you, you're gonna have to fix yourselves up a bit.'"

One worker on the place was regaling me with a story about the Navy Joes, and I was having a hard time following him until I realized that he was talking about the Navajo Indians.

12
Fun

People usually tend to think of Billy as a deadly serious person. And he is, but those who have observed him through the years have been privileged to see a personality which combines all of the desirable traits that go to make up a well-rounded person—not the least of which is a refreshing sense of humor.

One day Billy was in the living room of their home watching himself on a television program which had been pre-taped. The children were clattering up and down the uncarpeted stairs, shrieking like guinea hens and followed by barking dogs and scurrying cats. It sounded like an Apache uprising. Billy pleaded with Ruth, "Can't you please keep them quiet?" Then he added, deadpan, "If you don't mind, I'd like to hear what that man on TV has to say."

Billy once turned to a friend and said with a twinkle in his eye, "If Ruth tells you she's been using my toothbrush to clean her shoes, don't think she's kidding." (The friend said she couldn't understand why Billy felt he had to mention anything so obvious.)

Many have commented on the fact that Ruth has been

good medicine for Billy. She says of Billy's college days
that he was too serious, not even finding time to go to a
baseball game. This was a real shock to Ruth because her
Dad had at one time been a baseball pro. She said that
every date turned out to be either a preaching or religious
service of some kind. Yet she found, under all his dedica-
tion and depth, an irresistible winsomeness. Ruth also
recognized the fact that not only was Billy older in
chronological age than the other students; he was already a mature person in other ways, having his sights
set on definite goals and a determination not to be
sidetracked.

To balance this seriousness, God gave Billy a wife who
wouldn't seem out of place in a stained glass window, yet
who has enough humor to "prop him up on his leanin'
side" when burdens become so great one wonders if the
gaiety can ever survive the gloom. When Billy arrives
home, pressured as few men have been pressured, Ruth
takes her fun seriously, feeling that there are some
things "too important to be serious about." I'm reminded
of what Ruth's father said of her childhood, "An interesting mixture of deep spirituality and mischievous fun."
Christianity has never lobbied against wholesome laughter; the Bible says, "There is a time to weep and a time to
laugh" (Eccl. 3:4) and "A merry heart doeth good like a
medicine" (Prov. 17:22).

Ruth is not only able to laugh at herself, but there's a
noticeable upsurge in laughter when it has to do with any of
the staff or Billy. She loves to remind Billy about the time
they were invited to lunch at Clarence House in London.
When the dignified butler put out his hand to take Billy's
coat, Billy shook it vigorously. When Grady Wilson
was introduced to the Archbishop of Canterbury, whom he
should have addressed as "Your Grace," this dyed-in-
the-wood Baptist called him, "Brother Archbishop."

When Ruth was scheduled to be an attendant in an out-of-state wedding, she was planning to make the dress she was going to wear. But she was so bogged down with activities that the person engineering the wedding received a note from her, saying, "I'm going to have to cut out my dress on the plane and glue it on me when I get there." After she arrived, she and the others in the wedding party were discussing wedding thank-you notes. Ruth, at the time the mother of four children with another on the way, said, "That reminds me. As soon as I get home I'm going to have to start writing thank-you notes for the gifts Bill and I received for our wedding." One family has a prized picture of Ruth sitting on the floor painting the toenails of a bride-to-be.

One day Ruth had some of the staff up to lunch; the first course was consommé with meatballs, and all but one staff member was served this delicious appetizer. The victim was served muddy water with tadpoles in it, fresh from the pool. When he tried to stick his fork in a meatball, it swam away. Ruth felt that her offering was at least as appetizing as a delicacy that was once served Billy in a foreign country—mouse heads stuffed with ants.

On another occasion, Ruth had several women friends to dinner. Among them was an older friend who had dangerously high blood pressure, plus a serious heart condition, and her doctor had taken her off desserts. However, she kept insisting that Ruth give her a piece of blueberry pie along with everyone else. Ruth felt it would be tantamount to holding a loaded gun at her head, and she refused to serve her. The friend persisted, so Ruth finally left the table and in a few minutes was back with a hefty slice of pie, plus a mountain of whipped cream topping which the other guests didn't have. The guest started eating it, then looked quizzically at Ruth and put her fork down. The whipped cream had come out of Billy's pressurized shaving cream can.

Ruth is a neighborly sort of person and likes to share food, or whatever, so one of her neighbors was looking forward with anticipation to a tasty meal when she was handed a sack labeled, "Meat for your supper," which Ruth had sent down by a workman on the place. When she opened it up, a long, black, groggy snake slithered out. Ruth later said she thought she'd killed it; she'd only stunned it. Snakes abound in the area. Although, at the time, the Grahams had lived there only a few years, the man who worked on the place told me he'd already killed ninety-five rattlers. On one occasion, Ruth and a companion met a rattler face to face on the mountain. Ruth hit it with a large rock, then got in the jeep and ran over it with the wheels. But it took the addition of a wrench to kill it. She insisted that she didn't know whether she'd killed it or if it had died of a coronary from fright at hearing the companion scream.

One night T. W. Wilson, a staff member with the Billy Graham Evangelistic Association, called Ruth and in great excitement told her to rush to the yard and see a UFO in the sky near the mountain ridge. Ruth called Ned, who was the only one at home, and they hurried outside but could find nothing. Then Ruth realized it was the first of April. Unwilling to be bested by T. W., she told Ned to stay in the background and scream like a banshee while she called T. W. Getting him on the phone while Ned was furnishing the backdrop of screaming, Ruth shouted into the telephone, "It's landing in our yard!" and slammed down the receiver. Then she and Ned went out to sit on the steps and listen to T. W.'s car tires squealing as his car careened around the mountain curves hurling up the mountain, and braking to a sudden stop in the driveway. Ruth said sweetly, "April Fool" to T. W. and a companion he had with him. T. W. was incensed. He told Ruth that not only had he and his companion seen the UFO, but that several neighbors had also witnessed it. Finally, even Ruth was convinced they'd seen some strange object, but T. W. was still a little miffed. As he started home he said to Ruth from the car window, "Even if one should land in your yard, don't *call* me."

When one of Billy's secretaries was having a small party, one of the guests arrived dressed in her Sunday best. In the winter, the community is whistle-stop size and denim casual. (One resident reports that she saw a man go into the post office dressed in his pajamas and bathrobe and that she'd also seen a lady sitting in her car outside the post office in her nightgown.) The secretary was so impressed with the dressed-up guest that she went to the phone to alert Ruth, who is the tailored type. In about a half-hour, Ruth had everyone howling with laughter when she arrived at the party, dressed to the teeth, dripping in furs, lace flounces, and flowers, with jewelry coming out of her ears—necklaces, bracelets, earrings, and pins—a clotheshorse extravaganza.

For a good many years in Montreat, lot lines were often scrambled, with one owner not knowing where her line stopped and another's started. A friend of Ruth's had bought a lot and, though planning to build, wasn't quite ready to start. She was reduced to a severe case of nerves when she received a letter from Ruth, an excerpt of which follows: "Just a hurried note in case you haven't already heard. They're building on your property. I'm positive they haven't gotten permission, but they're notorious for that sort of thing. Do you want me to do anything about it?" (By this time the friend was a candidate for the hospital emergency room.) On the next page Ruth wrote,

"I'm not sure what they are—swallows or phoebes. But the nest is above your back living room window."

Writing to a prospective neighbor to tell her how the Graham house was progressing, Ruth said, "The reservoir is finished (except for the top), also the septic tank. Thought we should put it near enough to where you're going to build so that your boys can use the top of it for a skating rink."

Ruth's fun reaches all the way back to boarding-school days in Korea when she and a friend pulverized mothballs and poured the resulting mess into the salt shakers on the table. Obviously, the spaghetti lunch ended in the garbage cans. In looking back on the incident now, she regrets the waste of food.

A Montreat resident recalled the hymn sings held on Sunday evenings in the home, attended by the immediate family, grandparents, and, once in a while, a guest.

At one particular sing Billy was home and, of course, attended. He was singing his heart out, and Ruth whispered to the guest that he was off key. But the guest later said that she was so happy to be invited that she didn't notice his being off key. She concluded: "He sounded like Caruso to me."

A former secretary of Ruth's who, at the time, lived in the Graham home, kept notes as to what went on among the little Grahams and recently shared some of the stories with me as well as with Ruth and Billy. I hope they'll bring smiles to readers' faces as they did to the faces of the children's parents.

Little Anne said, "I *know* there is a Santa Claus 'cause I got a bracelet for Christmas that must have cost at least two dollars. And I *know* Mommie and Daddy couldn't afford that!"

Franklin spoke of "Menace the Dentist."

When GiGi went to Hampton DuBose School the first time, she carried in her suitcase an ample supply of socks. A few days later, she telephoned to ask her mother if she would send more socks. "What happened to all the socks you took with you?" inquired Ruth. "They're dirty," came the reply.

Once, when Ruth was out of town, Bunny told her grandmother on the phone that she wanted to come down to the valley for the night. "I know about everything on this mountain, and I'm looking for new places to sleep."

One day I walked into the kitchen and found Franklin playing with matches. "Franklin, you *know* your daddy told you not to play with matches," I scolded. "No, he didn't," insisted Franklin. "He told me not to let him *catch* me playing with matches." Then he said with a grin, "and I'm not going to let him catch me."

After delivering a little sermon, I asked, "Don't you think you should confess this to him?" "Heck, no!" replied Franklin. "He'd beat the dickens out of me."

Anne and her friend had seen the film *Tonka*. On the way home, I heard the most delightful conversation that went something like this:

Anne: "Did you see those muscles?"
Friend: "Whose? Sal Mineo's?"
Anne: "Oh, no! I meant the horse's."

When Bunny heard someone talking about Miss America, she asked, "Who is Miss America? Is she Uncle Sam's wife?"

She also remembers the fun the children had when Billy played the Spider Game with them, turning off all the lights in the house and chasing them through the darkened house.

One might wish that the laughter and mirth could continue unabated, but the world may have come upon the time to weep. In countless areas, laughter and mirth have given way to somber reflection as the world is seen teetering on the rim of disaster.

For many followers of Christ, the peals of laughter have been replaced by a deep and abiding joy as they remember that through Christ's sacrificial death on the cross, they no longer face heaven as aliens, and can join with little Anne Graham as she gratefully prayed at family devotions one morning, "Thank you, Lord, for coming to this dirty, dirty earth."

13
Travel

When the children were little, Ruth faced an almost impossible situation in trying to fairly divide her time between her husband and her children. There were always the critics that were parted down the middle, like hair. One group said of her traveling, "Poor children, no mother"; and if she stayed home with the children, they said, "Poor husband, no wife." (Many years ago the wife of a world-famous evangelist confessed to a friend, "My children are in hell today," giving as the reason that she had left them often in order to be on the travel circuit with her husband. This was of much concern to Ruth.)

In those days, when she was wrenched from the children, she felt like she was being "shipped overseas," and a friend has proof of the mother pangs in a letter she wrote during a foreign crusade. After writing that the crusades had been "marvelously blessed by God" she continued, "And shortly thereafter I head for home while Bill goes to the continent. And I can hardly wait. I'm so lonesome for the kiddies, I could die. But keeping busy and the thrilling work makes it all right."

In one letter from Europe, she told of planning to take the children and spend several months away from home, concluding, "Hate the thought"—then, "It's the best way to see Bill. But I'm weary of travel and would adore to stay put—as would the children."

But, consistently Ruth, she injects humor into any situation. Turning down an invitation to speak in Japan, she commented, "Why should I go halfway around the world to tell the Japanese women that they ought to stay home and take care of their children?"

Ruth said that because Billy was on the go so much of the time, it was hard for him to settle down after a crusade. It worried her when he'd come home and start talking about moving to the last place where a crusade had been held. She said she finally realized that he was just "talking," so she learned to let him talk it out and found he was more than content to stay where he was. (Strangely enough, in a recent study, Asheville, North Carolina, near their home, was pinpointed as the best all-around spot in the nation to live, of cities under 225,000.) The residents of Montreat love it, but most of them would agree that one of their number made a slip of the tongue and went too far when he announced at the Sunday service, "We will now worship Montreat with the morning offering."

Due to having to spend so much time traveling, Ruth quickly learned to shave any excesses in clothing. She'd take only a few travel-packable outfits. (Someone, knowing this, suggested giving her, for a going-away gift, a jar of all-purpose cream—for her face and coffee.)

Ruth was on one trip in Europe with the late Henrietta Mears, a wealthy Christian spinster who had also learned by trial and error how many outfits to leave at home. But on this trip, she and Ruth were invited to attend an affair that required an evening dress. Since she'd failed to take one with her, she fished out of her suitcase a pretty pink nightgown, stuck a slip under it, tied a sash around her waist, and she and Ruth were off for a night on the town.

In those days of so much going and coming, Ruth would leave just enough time to run under her hat and, as a friend expressed it, "Be off in a cloud of dust to the airport where she was soon airborne." Actually, she's never accompanied by a hat on her trips because the only time she took one, she says she lugged it in her hand all over Europe.

She'd come and go with lightning speed, touching down when you'd least expect her. One of her friends reported that she'd seen her in a hometown store shortly after she'd told her good-bye and seen her off on a plane to Europe. When she asked the reason for her hasty return, Ruth said, "I forgot my toothbrush."

On some occasions in those early days, Ruth would fly into New York from Europe or wherever, then take a train for home; and the children were almost beside themselves with joy when the train, bringing its precious cargo, was spotted down the tracks. At one of the home-comings, little Anne was jumping up and down, saying excitedly, "My heart's just giggling!"

Many friends may have felt a little twinge of envy as they envisioned the far-flung, exotic places that Ruth would see, but an excerpt from a letter to a friend gave a little different picture as to sightseeing: "I had three marvelous weeks with Bill (and T. W. and Grady . . . in southern France), followed them around 18 holes of golf everyday. If I ever want to go sightseeing, I shall have to marry someone else. But it was really good for me." (Ruth has always supported Billy's playing golf in order to get some exercise, which serves the purpose of counteracting the many hours he spends sitting in his study in sermon preparation.)

Billy has spent an incredible amount of time in planes and therefore has experienced all kinds of flying weather. He has admitted publicly that on one occasion during a dangerous flight, he experienced fear. The reason he gave his listeners was that he knew he was out of the will of God and that as soon as he got right with God, his fear was a thing of the past. However, it wasn't fear that made Billy say not too long ago that he'd be happy if he never saw another airport. And no wonder! It's been reported that Billy has been away from his family three-fourths of the time he and Ruth have been married. On one occasion, during a crusade in Europe, he opened his mail and found a picture of a small boy. He asked a staff member, "Who would be sending me such a large picture of their child?" He was told that it was his own son, Franklin. But turnabout is fair play because when he got home from that trip, Franklin asked his mother, "Who's him?"

One of Franklin's little friends happened to see Billy and Franklin together on one of Billy's times back at home and said, relieved, "Franklin *does* have a Daddy."

A guest at GiGi's ninth birthday celebration recalls Billy saying to her, "Would you believe this is the first birthday party of GiGi's I've ever attended?" He further added, pensively, "Wouldn't it be wonderful to be able to stay home with your family?" (Jesus offered a reward for what Billy has done, recorded in Mark 10:29-30: "There is no man that hath left house, or brethren, or sisters, or father, or mother, or wife, or children, or lands, for my sake, and the gospel's, But he shall receive an hundred-fold now in this time . . . and in the world to come eternal life.")

Billy has admitted publicly that there have been times when he's told Ruth good-bye with tears streaming down his face. Some would look on this as "bleeding on camera," but they forget that Christ shed tears in connection with the death of his friend, Lazarus, and also wept over Jerusalem.

But somehow the word got out that it was unmanly to cry, and even little boys have been inflicted with this lunacy.

The children had gone to a very sad Disney movie and had cried a good part of the way through it, and tears were still spilling over as they started for home. Little Franklin insisted to his sisters that he hadn't cried. When they pointed to the tears still on his face, a dead giveaway, he quickly brushed them away, saying, "I didn't know I was crying. I thought my eyes were bleedin'."

Ruth gives an inkling of the toll the "good-byes" have taken on her in a poem she wrote, "The Closing of a Door."

> We live a time secure,
> beloved and loving,
> sure
> it cannot last
> for long
> then—
> the goodbyes come
> again—again
> like a small death,
> the closing of a door.

One learns to live
with pain,
One looks ahead,
not back,
only before.
And joy will come again—
warm and secure—
If only for the now,
laughing,
We endure.[1]

The spiritual burdens surrounding the crusades are great. In the first days of travel when their transportation was by ship, Ruth recalls that friends brought the usual bon voyage gifts to their staterooms, including candy, fruit, and magazines. But one remembers her saying that she didn't have the heart to even open a magazine—that the trip over was spent in prayer and saturating herself with the words of the Bible. Ruth knows that a great faith comes only through the words of Scripture as Romans 10:17 says, "Faith cometh by hearing, and hearing by the Word of God." That is why both she and Billy feel that the memorization of Scripture is all-important.

Ruth's letters about the crusades show that Billy's work is as important to her as it is to him. From London a letter was received: "These meetings have been absolutely wonderful. I ate with some folks concerned with the theatre yesterday and they cannot figure how Harringay is packed night after night (ten weeks now) and places like the theatre, where the smash hit Russian ballerinas are dancing, isn't even filled. I explained the two reasons. 1. Humanly, there is a spiritual hunger in the hearts of the people. 2. Spiritually, God is answering prayer. And I have never heard of such a volume of prayer the world over. Night after night we see the results—not in crowds but in individuals reached and transformed by the power of Christ."

Then an enthusiastic letter from Scotland. Ruth whisks you up and away and sets you down in the middle of plans for that crusade: "I wish I could tell you how God is opening the way in Scotland. Such interest! Such expectancy! The cooperation is unbelievable." She goes on to detail the exciting happenings—then puts in an earnest plea: "Do keep praying . . . that God will move in a very deep way."

Ruth's great faith in prayer comes from her secure belief in the promises of God's word that "He who cometh to God must believe that he is, and that he is a rewarder of them that diligently seek him" (Heb. 11:6).

Much of the spiritual turnaround being experienced by vast segments of the population the world over can be traced to the flowering of the seeds planted by Billy's crusades all through the years.

In 1980 Ruth and a brother and sister took a trip to their old homeplace in China. She wrote in a letter, "Yes, the trip to our old home was unforgettable. I even found the little Chinese house in which I was born. Most of the buildings in our station are still standing, all run down but used for various things from wholesale grocery outlets to dormitory space. Thank God, his work is in changed lives, not buildings. One Christian said, 'The seed your father sowed is still bearing fruit.' Most of the older Christians are dead, but the younger ones are carrying on. God is in control. Bill is in Alberta, but I know he would want to join me in sending love." Billy had insisted that a photographer accompany the family in order to bring back photographs which would later be shown in churches and on television.

In a lighter vein, Billy and Ruth were on a train in Europe and got into conversation with a passenger who was on his way to a convention. Ruth asked him why he wasn't taking his wife along. He answered, "When you're going to a banquet, you don't take a sandwich in your pocket." Ruth wrote home, "Just call me a sandwich."

When Billy was having a crusade in Africa, young Bunny had been absorbed by a sad news account of a man killing his wife. After saying that she was glad her daddy had come from a Christian home, she quickly dispensed with her worries by saying, "But even if he hadn't, he's way down in Africa where he can't hurt anybody."

Billy thrives in a sunny climate while Ruth is a willing hostage to snow. An excerpt from a letter while traveling: "It's wonderful here but I miss being snowed in." She went on to say that they were heading for New Zealand the next day. No matter how maddening the relentless snow is to others, to Ruth, it's heaven-sent. She loves it for herself (but not for those for whom it causes suffering).

Ethel and Lucy of the "I Love Lucy" series were in a whipped-cream resort—snow as far as the eye could see. Ethel, overwhelmed, said to Lucy, "Isn't it beautiful?" Lucy answered, bored, "If you like white."

Ruth likes white. And because she feels a need for isolation in order to accomplish the myriad of unfinished tasks ahead of her, she'd be jubilant if, only temporarily, she could face complete abandonment in a snow prison in their mountain home.

Note

1. From Ruth Bell Graham, *Sitting by My Laughing Fire*, copyright © 1977 by Ruth Bell Graham; used by permission of Word Books, Publisher, Waco, Texas 76796.

14
Thoughtfulness of Parents and Children

There were no television cameras moving in to record the daily "nice guy," thoughtful approach that Billy and Ruth have taken with people through the years; but the appreciative recipients of their kindnesses remember, though some prefer to keep their experiences under wraps as too personal to be told.

There's space for only a few of the hundreds, but these show the trend of their lives.

The Grahams were friends in need to an elderly man who had been grossly mistreated. When they found he had nowhere to live in his declining, ailing years, they insisted that he move into their attractive, renovated cabin and live out his years there. The first Sunday after he arrived, a friend of Ruth's saw him at church. With grateful tears in his eyes and a voice brimming with emotion, he told her, "I've come home!" Ruth saw to it that he got to Sunday School and church every Sunday. Though he could cook, she often fixed and took him his meals; and when the family ate out on Sundays, he was included as a family member. She also had a large photograph made of him and hung it in a place of honor in the family room, where it remained long after his death.

163

It still hangs in the upstairs hall "gallery of memories."

One day a visitor went to the Graham home and found Ruth in the kitchen, cradling a strange baby in one arm, fixing breakfast with her free hand, and trying to shut the oven door with her foot. The baby's parents were young missionaries home on furlough and were desperate for sleep because of the travel-worn, upset baby. So Ruth had taken the baby into her room for an all-night stand while the parents caught up on their sleep.

When one of the Grahams's friends was in the hospital for a serious operation, Ruth not only sent him a gift the first day; but day after day gifts would arrive, for the most part inexpensive, gay things to lift the spirits—but always something that showed care and thought. After his death, she told his bereaved wife, "If you need to get away, I'll drop everything and go with you anywhere."

A friend reports that one summer she opened her home in Montreat to find that Ruth and her mother had bought material for curtains for the entire house, made them, and hung them on rods which they'd also bought and installed. As an added bonus, Ruth had found out the approximate time of her arrival and had gone back to turn on the electric blanket.

One Montreat resident tells that when she and her son came down with the flu, Ruth and the children came down the mountain to their home. While the patients were feebly protesting, Ruth pulled them bodily out of bed and took them home, where they were given intensive care and cheerful round-the-clock room service until they were on foot again. She adds, "Ruth could have used the excuse that she also had Billy in bed with the flu, but that would never have occurred to her."

On one occasion, when Ruth found that a friend was temporarily on the sick list, she had her brought to their home and, as Bunny said, "bed-fed her" with a gourmet soup which she herself had made. Then she waited on her hand and foot—later coming to her room in her robe to read the Bible and pray with her. The friend commented, "There was nothing unusual in that because Ruth has always been a selfless type of person; the thing that lifted it out of the ordinary was the fact that, unknown to me, the paper that day had reported that Ruth had been forced to cancel her trip to Liberia with Mrs. Nixon and Billy because she was too ill to go."

Ruth is also thoughtful in the so-called "little areas," though that is a misnomer. Sometimes these areas give an even clearer insight into a person's character. A visitor in the Graham home tells of mentioning a certain book that she was interested in reading—then of leaving and going to a nearby tearoom to have lunch with friends. She says, "I'd forgotten all about the book when I looked up and saw Ruth, a vision in yellow wool, coming through the door of the tearoom with the book in her hand." Although she was scheduled to meet Billy's plane arriving from Europe, she'd clocked the time she had left, then gone through the maze of books in the home until she'd put her hand on the one in question.

A friend of Ruth's was having a few friends in for refreshments but purposely didn't invite Ruth because she knew Billy was home for their wedding anniversary. Halfway through the afternoon, Ruth came to the door, saying she was crashing the party—and in her hands she carried their beautiful anniversary cake, with only a few small slices missing.

When one of Ruth's friends was being given a book autograph party, Ruth was standing by. When the line of people became skimpy, with too many empty spaces, Ruth would suddenly remember "a friend" that she'd forgotten to put on her list to buy a book for, and she'd step back in line. The friend for whom the autograph party was given also jokingly accused Ruth of going through the line several times more, disguised in different wigs. Ruth went beyond the call of duty to make the total attendance more impressive.

From a letter to a neighbor: "Bunny, Anne, and Bill walked up past your house this week. Bill's gone now, but Bunny and Anne said your road isn't washed out. I'll check it to see, and will tend to getting it fixed if it is—so don't worry. The bad weather about ruined our road. The pavement looks as if it exploded in spots."

A summer resident recalls another incident of the thoughtfulness of the Graham children. In a letter from her teenage son who had arrived in Montreat in advance of his parents, he wrote, "The cabin was a mess. There was a bird's nest over your bed with four eggs in it. GiGi and Anne are cleaning it for me."

One woman recalled a particularly magnanimous thing Billy had done. When he arrived home from Vietnam where he'd spent Christmas with the troops and where both of her sons were stationed, he called her to say, "I've just gotten home, but I knew you'd want to know that I had both of your sons meet me in Saigon. I had dinner with them." He also brought photographs of them taken with him and T. W. Wilson (who, the boys said, "looked just like a younger Bob Hope").

One of the boys, writing about it, said, "We got a big kick out of seeing Billy Graham and talking to him. I will always thank him for that kindness, especially at a time of the year that was most difficult for me." The other wrote glowingly, and also mentioned the thrill of riding on a Honda behind Billy's official car. Since he was sent by the president, he had a four-star rating. To add to the glow of it all, the woman said that Ruth, in a sort of "hands across the sea" gesture, had invited her to share Christmas dinner with them.

A former secretary of Ruth's recently wrote to her, "I remember how you all made me feel like a part of the family, and how much that meant to me then, and still does. I will never forget all the precious little things the children did for me—the little notes, the hugs, the reassurance of their love, the times they would call the office just to say hello. One of my sweetest memories was of the several times I took a train trip. As I started to get on the train in Black Mountain, the children handed me little bouquets of wild flowers they had picked along the tracks. No flowers on earth could have been more precious to me."

She continued, "One Sunday morning Billy had not felt like accompanying his family to the church service. When they were returning home they found him waiting by the pool with a picnic lunch in hand. The children were all hungry, so a surprise picnic was especially welcome. GiGi opened the sack of food and counted out the peanut butter and jelly sandwiches. There was one for each. And, if I recall correctly, there was also a can of pork and beans.

"Just as it was time to pass out the sandwiches, an old car came chugging up the road past all the 'private property' signs. The car's radiator was overheated; and as it approached the swimming pool, the smoke was beginning to rise from the hood. Billy went down to investigate, and this, of course, meant a delay in eating. (Not good news for four hungry children!) He could be heard talking to the embarrassed occupants of the car, expressing his concern and asking if he could do anything to help. And he enthusiastically invited them to 'Come on up and share our picnic lunch. There's plenty of food for everyone.' (Or words to that effect.)

"About that time, four little Grahamses began to look more than a little worried. By then, however, Ruth had begun to assure the children there really *was* plenty, for sharing always made a picnic more fun, and so on. The folks declined the gracious invitation, got their car turned around, and headed back down the mountain; but I am sure they left with a feeling of being loved.

"While the delay might have slowed down the consumption of peanut butter and jelly sandwiches, it afforded the children a valuable look at the total unselfishness of their parents and of how they work together as a team to share the love of Jesus—whether it involves a crusade with many people or just two or three embarrassed folks who found themselves in the wrong place at the wrong time."

15

Ruth and Young People

Now and then the Billy Graham Evangelistic Association pays for speakers at Montreat Anderson College, near the Graham home.

One time it was Brother Andrew, better known as "God's Smuggler" because of his successful forays into Communist countries to distribute Bibles.

Ruth was elected to meet his plane. When asked if she were sure she'd recognize him, she assured the committee that she would.

But later, on the platform with him, she admitted to the students that she'd missed him. She said, "I was looking for a fat, saintly Dutchman." The students laughed. They could see that he was slim and handsome, with no outward signs of saintliness. Ruth then told the students that she'd asked him how he wanted to be introduced. He answered, "Either as a missionary or 'God's Smuggler.'" Ruth said, "I decided that college students would rather listen to a smuggler than a missionary." Accordingly she presented the man who, when he'd enter a Communist country, would pray that Christ, who had once made blind eyes see, would now make seeing eyes blind so that his Word could be given to people experiencing a famine of Bibles. He said that anyone could get into a Communist country if they weren't particular about getting out.

Young people are attracted to Ruth, not only because she's attractive but because they know she'll fight for them at the drop of a hat. A case in point was a tough city gang leader. Ruth went all out to help him, but he backslid so often that everybody but Ruth was ready to throw in the towel. "He's hopeless," they'd say in disgust. But she looked at them granite-faced and insisted that the payoff would come.

On New Year's morning some years ago, an all-night guest in the house was at the breakfast table. Ruth, a little bleary-eyed, told her that at a few minutes after midnight, the phone by her bed had rung. She confessed she was so groggy from sleep that she'd groped around, even trying to pick up the clock radio to answer it. Finally she'd come to life enough to connect with the phone. It was this "hopeless" boy on the line, wishing her a Happy New Year and telling her that he was enrolled in Columbia Bible College and on his way to becoming a minister. Ruth asked, "Can you think of a better way to start the new year?"

Nothing seems to be too much trouble for Ruth when it concerns young people.

On one occasion, eighteen young people dropped by the Graham home unexpectedly. Ruth fixed a meal for them and sent them on their way rejoicing.

One afternoon she was entertaining a group of young people—children of foreign missionaries who had come to the United States for their college education. She looked really "used up" and bone weary, so much so that an older guest insisted that she should rest. Ruth replied, her face glowing, "I'm not tired. I feel like I'm entertaining royalty!"

Ruth has endless fun in dealing with young people. In one of her wackier moments she sent a young man off to school with forty pictures of himself—from wallet to less than mural size—all in the same pose. He told her he put all of them up in his room and invited the student body in for open house.

Both Ruth and Billy tried to teach the children the value of money and refused to dole it out indiscriminately to them.

On one occasion when Franklin didn't have even pocket change, he asked Ruth to give him some money. She said bluntly, "Go *earn* it," which proved unfortunate for one of Ruth's friends, who was parked on the side of the road out of gas.

Chuckling, she said that Franklin happened by and, seeing her predicament, refused to budge until she paid him for the gas and also included a generous kickback. She laughingly referred to the incident as one of her first experiences with price gouging.

Eventually Franklin became a young person himself, and Ruth's desire for him, as well as for all young people, was "to stand without being hitched."

After having talked to him about certain concerns until she was blue in the face, with no outward results, Ruth finally asked him to tell her how she could get his cooperation. He said, "Say it *once!*"

As one little boy said of one mother, "She talks more than I can hear." Ruth said in her book *It's My Turn,* "I talk my children dizzy."[1]

During one school year, one of Ruth's college-age friends arrived in Montreat with several of his fraternity brothers and settled themselves in his parents' summer cabin. Soon afterward Ruth wrote his mother: "That crazy Tommy, like the foolish virgins, didn't check the oil heater and it went out the night the temperature went down to nine degrees. Of course, I didn't give them much sympathy as all they would have to have done was to come up here and crowd into three empty bedrooms."

Probably the most-used expression young people hold to in describing Ruth is, "She's my best friend."

Two boys living near her loved her so much that they paid her the zenith of all compliments. They named their dog for her (and partly for the woman who had given it to them—in both cases, Ruth).

One day one of the boys came in the house laughing. He said he'd been calling his dog, "Here, Ruth, here, Ruth" at the top of his lungs; and far up the mountain, Ruth had answered, "Coming!"

From some accounts, either oral or written, some might get the idea that Ruth spends her time hurtling through life, engaging in death-defying feats. This is a caricature of her. She's anything but flaky. There's usually hard reasoning behind what she does.

At one time, a young friend of hers had bought a motorcycle, bringing down the wrath of his family on his head. Ruth, finally feeling that enough had been said (his family agreeing), decided that he needed some concrete backing. So she told him, truthfully, "I've always wanted to own one. How about taking me for a ride on it?" He agreed to it with the proviso that she'd get a black turtleneck sweater and black goggles to hide behind, which she did. But she added ruefully, "People will recognize my nose, no matter what."

After riding behind her young friend for a while, she asked him to let her go it alone. She got on the motorcycle and headed down the highway. Everything went with computerized accuracy until she tried to stop it. She'd forgotten to ask how, so she throttled it down to a slow walk; it stumbled along until it finally fell over and she fell down a slight incline with the motorcycle close behind.

A big, burly, tattooed truck driver saw the spill, brought his big truck to a screeching halt, and rushed to help her. She thanked him and told him that if he'd just turn the motorcycle around, get her on it, and head it down the highway, she'd be OK. She said, undaunted, "My instructor's down the road and he'll help me get stopped."

Shortly after this, the young man himself fell off the motorcycle and hurt himself enough for Ruth to put him to bed under Billy's heat lamp and then let him talk things out. If a person has bruises of the spirit, along with physical bruises, Ruth has an uncanny perceptiveness to know it and bring it to the surface. One woman whose spirits were at half-mast, and whose stars had fallen out of her sky, said of Ruth, "She made me want to open my Bible again."

I've heard Ruth say, "*Pray* and *listen*." She has a rare insight into troubled souls and few, if any, who have come to her for help have experienced a dry run.

One of Ruth's friends was having a rough time decoding the accent of one of the little Graham grandchildren who had been born in a foreign country and spoke English with an accent. He became increasingly disgusted with her failure to understand him and said in disdain, "God no give you no ears!" He gave ears to Ruth. Someone has said, "There's a way of listening that surpasses all compliments." Ruth has discovered that way. She "listens between the lines."

In counseling young people, she seems almost to devour their problems, many of which are serious. Some have lost sight of almost every vestige of their faith in college. Though she might not express it this way, she wouldn't consider it "petty larceny" when a young person's faith is stolen. She would consider it grand theft, and she sets to work to restore it.

Ruth says to young people or anyone with ears to hear: "There are three things you can count on: That two and two are four—that I'll never divorce Bill—and that the Bible is the Word of God."

When Ruth finds the lives of young people in a topsy-turvy, snarled condition, she's always able to point them to the Bible. She can and does point to her own life as proof that tangled lives can become smooth again. There was a brief but traumatic time when the only thing Ruth was sure of was that there was a God. She says that all the time she was arguing against the things she'd always believed (and strongly believes now), she was, in reality, crying for help—pleading for someone to convince her she was wrong. She recognizes that same desperation in some of the young people to whom she talks. She knows that by pointing them to the living, indwelling Christ of the Bible, out of the thick black doubt will come a faith as strong as that of doubting Thomas of the Bible—or her own.

If a young person has chosen an evil and destructive path, giving as his reason, "Everybody does it," Ruth can point him to God's words "Thou shalt not follow a multitude to do evil" (Ex. 23:2).

Ruth's infectious courage is well known to young people. She agrees wholeheartedly with the young man who said, "I'm tired of being one of the chicken majority."

If it's a book that needs vents in its covers, Ruth doesn't hesitate to say so. If it's alcohol or other drugs which are threatening to make derelicts out of young people, she doesn't hesitate to go on TV with the sheriff of the county to say so. On one occasion, when a certain nation claimed that its crime rate had gone down, Ruth reminded listeners that certain crimes had been decriminalized and were no longer called crimes.

The largest Pro-Life organization was formed in the Graham home. Interestingly, a greatly admired black woman, the late Ethel Waters, a very devoted friend of the Grahams, who blessed the world with her voice and faithful commitment to Christ, was the product of a rape. Her mother was the victim of a rapist.

In mounting frenzy, the creation *versus* evolution question is making headlines around the world, with many United States taxpayers, including Billy, feeling that if evolution is taught in the public schools, creation should also be taught, giving students the right to study both the creation and evolution models in order to decide which to them seems the most plausible. Around thirty years ago, I remember Ruth taking the biblical stand that reproduction is "after his kind" or "after its kind," pounding in the words. Not too long ago, that conclusion was reached on a television report of an experiment dealing with the fruit fly. Viewers were made aware of the fact that in spite of every kind of experiment to make the fruit fly something else, it's still a fruit fly. A recent NBC poll showed 86 percent of the population favoring creation being taught alongside evolution.

Ruth has often taught the Bible lesson on Sundays to college students. She spruces up her teaching with down-to-earth cracker-barrel wisdom and illustrations. I remember her using as an illustration their mountain contractor, who had very little formal education but who knew things that many educated people would give their eyeteeth to know. She quoted his version of the Bible verse, "Whom the Lord loveth, He 'chaseth,'" instead of chasteneth. And that, in effect, is what Christ taught in his story of the lost coin, the lost sheep, and the prodigal son. His search for the lost continues.

When Hitler threw Martin Niemöller into a concentration camp, a less brave minister visited him there and with a wringing-of-hands attitude asked, "Martin Niemöller, why are *you* here?" Niemöller looked him in the eye and asked, "Why are you *not* here?" It's doubtful if anyone will ever have to ask Ruth that question.

Note

1. From *It's My Turn* by Ruth Bell Graham copyright © 1982 by Ruth Bell Graham. Published by Fleming H. Revell Company. Used by permission.

16

Friends

Anyone who knows Ruth knows that she has no "best friend" but Christ, but there are many all over the world who claim friendship with her: rich and poor, tall and short, old and young, fat and slim. Her heart is made of a stretch material that takes in all types in all races.

Some, because of her position, have a tendency to genuflect; others are more or less cut on the bias. One of this type said, "We've had many glorious years agreeing and disagreeing on a thousand and one subjects."

Ruth doesn't expect a person to always agree with her in order to claim her friendship. (She's even said that if a husband and wife agree on everything, one of them is unnecessary.) And when disagreements arise between her and a friend, she doesn't take the attitude of one little boy who said, "I have only *one* friend, and I *hate him*." Rather, she'd laughingly agree with one of her little grandsons who, after his parents had been arguing, said to them, "Shake hands, you guys, and make up!"

One morning Ruth and one of her more mulish friends were having a spirited conversation in the Graham home. As their voices became louder and more high pitched, one of the little girls looked up from her play and asked, "Are you two fightin'?" Calling a truce in the still-unsolved argument, Ruth said descriptively to the friend, "Calming you down when you're upset is like trying to put out a volcano with a candle snuffer." Then she added, "But we can yell and holler to our heart's content and we understand each other perfectly." After one particularly bombastic session this friend found a poem in her mailbox, headed: *Dedicated To You*—the gist of which was that she hated arguing with a person who was immovable but sweet. She contended that she didn't get as hot under the collar with people who yelled—because, then, she could holler.

Ruth doesn't holler, but gratefully she's no Casper Milquetoast; and as one friend says, chuckling, "She can pin your ears back if the occasion demands." At one time this friend was upset over what she called the "claptrap drivel" her acquiescing son was being taught at college, and the son wanted Ruth to intervene to get his mother off his back. The mother said that Ruth paved the way for giving her advice by saying humorously, "I can always be objective when it comes to *your* children."

This same friend was laughing as she recalled a letter she'd once received from Ruth, beginning with the words: "We've been friends long enough to level with each other," and she was still chuckling as she continued, "Then Ruth really let me have it—blast, blast. She accurately pointed out that I was mishandling the situation with my son. But, typical Ruth, she was gracious enough, humorous enough, and farseeing enough to add a postscript: 'Keep this letter five years and send it back as advice to me.'" Later, still concerned over the way the mother was handling the situation but wanting to mollify her and give her an "E" for effort, plus assuring that it would all work out for the good, Ruth said encouragingly, "I'm sure you talked with him all the way as you drove him back to school." The mother said, "No, I didn't; I yelled at him all the way." Ruth said dryly, "I know; he told me." She later wrote the son, "Your mom's praying more and yelling less."

Giving a description of one of her more zealous friends, Ruth wrote: "She would not only gladly die for her faith, but she'd cheerfully kill a few others in the process."

There was always the banter that went on between Ruth and her friends. After Ruth had been the platform speaker at a large gathering of women, a friend was heard to say to her, "Either I've improved or you saw me come in, because you didn't use me as an illustration of one of the bad guys as you usually do in your speeches."

Ruth is a sweet person, but those who know her well would say that it's never a cloying sweetness.

However, I checked some of the ways she's signed letters to friends through the years, and after hearing Franklin say, "My mother is fiesty," I was also reminded of her many-faceted personality when I read her words "signing off" in letters: "This is just to say I love you"; "Love you loads"; "You'll never know how much I love you."

Ruth's time is severely rationed, but in spite of her demanding schedule the words most often heard from her by a friend who might need her help are "I'll *take* time."

When the children were small, people would show their interest in Billy and Ruth by sending large amounts of candy to the children. One day Ruth appeared at a friend's home, bearing sacks of candy and saying, "I brought this candy for your kids; it gives mine cavities."

Ruth is never far away from her Bible because so much of it is stored in her memory. Its words are an integral part of her life, and there are few occasions when Ruth can't make the conversation richer by the addition of a Bible verse. One day a friend and Ruth were lazily talking. The friend said, "I get a little tired of hearing people say, 'Praise the Lord.'" (She later explained that she wanted the expression to be sincere, not just repetitious words.) Ruth didn't say anything, but handed her companion a letter which had some very good news in it for her. As she read the letter, the friend suddenly burst out, "Well, praise the Lord!" Ruth smiled and said, "Out of the fullness of the heart, the mouth speaketh."

The person is fortunate who, when going through a time of sorrow or testing, can count Ruth among her friends. One such person recalled a letter she'd received from her during such a time. Ruth had written, "I'm sitting here beside the fire in solitary bliss. No one's home but me, and for a change it's pure luxury." After expressing several things on her mind as to the friend's concern, Ruth continued, "And in case you're stewing, remember 'In NOTHING be anxious and fret not, it leads only to evil' and 'Commit thy way unto the Lord, trust also in him, and he SHALL bring it to pass.' I don't care what you're worrying about, worrying is a sin because over and over the Lord tells us not to.

"I've been sitting here listening to Henrietta Mears on a record and Psalm 37:5 was her favorite verse. So I've been going over my worries and pointedly committing each one. It really lifts the load. Only with me, it's got to become an attitude as well as an act. We're praying."

In another letter to a friend, this sentence stands out: "Look back on your life. Has the Lord ever failed you? He's not going to start now." To impress on one friend the futility of worrying she wrote: "What have you been worrying about lately? I'm running a little low on ideas myself. How about sharing a few?" If Ruth's friends were asked to pick one habit in Ruth's day-to-day living that has impressed them most, I believe it would be the fantastically cheerful way she always answers the phone, no matter how many times a day she has to answer it. If anyone has ever detected a cross or strained note in her voice, they haven't come forward to report it.

As is well known, Ruth never burdens others with her problems. But one friend recalled that Ruth once said to her, "Pray for us," which is an entirely different category. She wasn't asking help from the friend; she was asking help from God, and was only following Christ's words in Matthew 18:19: "If two of you shall agree on earth as touching anything that they shall ask, it shall be done for them of my Father which is in heaven." Because the answer was swift in coming, the friend was reminded of God's promise in Isaiah 65:24: "Before they call, I will answer; and while they are yet speaking, I will hear." Prayer is like breathing to Ruth. And she doesn't hesitate to ask friends to join with her to prove God's promises. One friend said that Ruth wrote her, "Let's remember to pray for one another and one another's children. They are the Lord's too."

A friend said, "You can tell Ruth anything." Perhaps the best way to describe her would be to describe her in the words of an Arabian proverb: "A friend is one to whom one may pour out all the contents of one's heart, chaff and grain together, knowing that the gentlest of hands will take and sift it, keep what is worth keeping, and with the breath of kindness blow the rest away."

17
Criticism—Pro and Con

As concerns criticism, Abraham Lincoln, when he was President of the United States, said, "If I were to read, much less answer, the attacks made on me, this shop might as well be closed for another business. I do the very best I know how—the very best I can, and I mean to keep doing so until the end. If the end brings me out wrong, ten angels swearing I was right, would make no difference."

And having in mind both critics and fans, he declared, "The shepherd drives the wolf from the sheep's throat for which the sheep thanks the shepherd as his liberator while the wolf denounces him for the same act. Plainly the sheep and the wolf are not agreed on a definition of liberty."

Ruth was looking at a picture of herself in a national magazine that made her look like a sick duck. She commented cheerfully, "They took a hundred pictures of me in order to get one bad enough to print."

Billy is no stranger to criticism either. Before he became an evangelist, he was a top-flight Fuller brush salesman, and one day an irate woman dumped water on him from her second story window.

In the days before Billy reached the status he now enjoys (and suffers), and before he was listened to by anyone but the masses, reporters, rightly feeling their responsibility to expose any lurking phoniness in this new prophet on the scene, would sometimes ask him a trick question (the method that was used to try to trick Christ).

Ruth and a companion were in the living room of the Graham home, watching on television as one of this type interviewed Billy.

The friend admitted that her nerves were leaping like fresh water trout for fear Billy would be painted into a corner. The reporter asked Billy a question that seemed to defy an answer. He answered it easily and without fanfare. Ruth was silent for a moment, then turned to her companion and said, "You and I both know Bill's not that smart. That was God." She always said that when Billy was pushed against the ropes by an antagonist, "God really helps that man." And she doesn't hesitate to give every shred of glory to God, saying, "They don't know who they're fighting!"

Billy has said the same thing in different words as he's reiterated time and time again, "If the Holy Spirit ever took his hands off me, my lips would turn to clay."

Christian listeners on the Phil Donahue Show felt that God must have helped Billy with some of his answers that day. When Donahue said, "Let's pretend I'm at one of your crusades," Billy elicited laughter from the audience when he said, "Don't pretend, come!"

When Donahue asked Billy if he prayed for the Johnny Carson Show, Billy said, "I pray for yours, too." Laughter rippled over the audience, and a surprised grin appeared on Donahue's face.

Sometimes Billy had criticism from his own children.

One of the little girls, watching him on television and hearing him thunder like Jeremiah, complained to her mother, "Why does he talk so *mean* to them?"

But the youngest little girl, who Ruth said was "a character," felt that sinners had it coming to them. So she wrote from Europe to two of her mother's friends: "We had a save trip . . . were all find except . . . little homesick and miss you. Daddy was the only Evanlistic man in the meeting. We were praying, and he belt them. Well, better close—love you both. Miss you xxxxxxx (kisses)."

Later she wrote in regard to plans to come home, "nowing Daddy, we may come by sub."

One of the little girls was greatly worried when Billy was hospitalized for a while and said worriedly to her mother, "Just think of all the people not gettin' saved!"

When the older son was in high school, his mother asked him what he'd do if he heard anyone criticizing his dad. He said, "It would depend on how big he was."

Criticism comes from many sources. Through the years there's been a fundamentalist school which one would think would be in Billy's camp but which has consistently blackballed him.

One of the little Graham girls rushed to a neighbor's house, her eyes as big as portholes and almost choking with excitement at the earthshaking news she was bearing. Naming the school, she fairly exploded with indignation and disbelief and said, "Do you know that they'll expel you at that school if you even eat a Graham cracker?"

Ruth told of a TV station in Europe with fairly wide coverage, the owner of which was interviewing Billy. Perhaps thinking that Billy had gone into evangelism with dollar signs in his eyes, he asked Billy if he minded telling the viewing audience what his salary was. Billy said without hesitation, "Not if you don't mind telling them what yours is." Ruth said the station immediately blacked out.

On one occasion, eager to get a scoop on what took place when Billy and Ruth were entertained by Queen Elizabeth and Prince Philip, one reporter even broke down the door to Billy's hotel room. All he got was a "No comment" (and probably a bill from the hotel).

Ruth tells of other eager reporters, one saying that Billy, when he was in London, had patted Prince Charles's head; she said he didn't even see Prince Charles.

Another report came out that the Grahams's oldest son was going to marry Lena Horne's daughter. Ruth said that he was eleven years old at the time and that the reporter had later retracted the story. Consequently, Ruth has stayed warily watchful, though much of the time she feels they've had a fair press.

On one occasion a friend commented on the fact that a certain interviewer seemed to be so pleasant and considerate. Ruth, grinning, said, "All the time he's smiling, he's probably writing, 'She has a nose like an anteater.'"

Years ago Ruth wrote a letter to a friend in which she said: "We're hoping and praying the fifth little Graham will be nice enough to arrive before Bill leaves for the Caribbean and between all his intervening engagements. We *think* within the next seven days. The little cradle is all fixed and ready and we can hardly wait."

When certain people found out that Ruth had used her wedding veil to decorate the cradle, she was soundly taken to task for not being sentimental.

She wrote a friend, "How could a person possibly use it in a more sentimental way," concluding, "I'm up to the cap now."

Billy has been criticized for appearing on questionable talk shows, but he cites cases of listeners who have accepted Christ on hearing him. He reminds people that Christ was also criticized for associating with questionable folk. Billy knows that there will always be pen pals who turn out to be poison pen pals. According to the Bible, criticism is to be expected by a follower of Christ.

Billy has been criticized for saying to new converts, "Go to the church of your choice," but it's been noted in several of his *My Answer* columns that he's told his readers to go to a church where the Bible is believed and preached and where Christ is exalted as the *only* way of salvation—which should satisfy the most critical of his accusers.

Even ministers haven't always given Billy the gentle-dove treatment. One day several of them were feeding him to the lions, and one of them, the minister of the largest church represented, who had also joined in the roasting, finally said refreshingly, "Why don't we just admit what our trouble is: we're just jealous." And before this minister died he said, "My wife and I listen to Billy every chance we get."

However, on another occasion, a minister, known even among ministers for his "suffocating mediocrity" on the job, said pompously about Billy, "I don't like anything about him!"

Some of the most vitriolic of Billy's critics, after meeting him in person, made a right about-face. One critic, after meeting him, had the look of someone caught drowning little puppies and exclaimed, "He was nearest the spirit of my Lord's of anyone I ever met."

Billy has at times criticized himself, recalling a few happenings of his earliest ministerial days that he felt were foolish. But most of those who love him, on hearing about them, only love him more. For instance, Billy admits to loving color, and he feels that the God he serves is a daring decorator. But he says that the wildly painted ties he wore in the pulpit in those early days must have been a source of embarrassment to his parents. He's also admitted that he wishes he could recall some statements that he's made. (In other words, he's human.)

Ruth has often criticized herself. After writing about "an everyday growing and knowing Christ, and a day-by-day experiencing of his compassion and transforming power," she added, "But I pray for you and me, especially me. I live so in the shallows instead of launching out into the deep. I am such an expert at loafing when I should be up and at it." As for Ruth living in the shallows and loafing, her friends would say, "Ridiculous!" She puts countless people to shame with her diversified accomplishments.

In Ruth's book *It's My Turn* she has opened to readers some early entries in her diary and says she has kept her promise to tell the truth, "Whether bitter or sweet, salty, or even peppery." She confessed in the diary:

"I am a weak, lazy, indifferent character; casual where I should be concerned; concerned where I should be carefree; self-indulgent, hypocritical, begging God to help me when I am hardly willing to lift a finger for myself; quarrelsome where I should be silent, silent where I should be outspoken; vacillating, easily distracted and sidetracked."[1]

One finds, upon reading the biographies of great men and women, that the nearer they are to God, the more heinous their sins appear to them. In their own eyes, their relationship to God is anything but worthy.

As I read Ruth's criticism of herself, I recalled that during the Middle Ages in a certain village in England, it was the custom to brand in the forehead of a criminal the letters designating his crime. One such man was branded with the letters ST for sheep thief.

Later he was converted to Christ, and from then on led an exemplary and Christlike life.

Many years passed, and a stranger arrived in the village. Noting the then faintly discernible letters in the man's forehead, he asked a villager what they meant. The villager thought a moment and said, "I don't remember"—then, "Oh, yes, I remember, they stand for 'Saint.'"

Ruth, in protesting some of the nice things said about her in this book, told me they made her think of the man who mistakenly asked Beverly Shea to sing for him the song, "How Great I Am." (This majestic song, "How Great Thou Art," continues to bring out the "awesome wonder" in hundreds of thousands of people as Beverly Shea and countless other voices join in to take its rapturous praise of Almighty God to the ends of the earth.)

Leafing through some old issues of both *Christian Century* and *Christianity Today*, it was interesting to find how the criticisms of Billy's trip to Moscow were handled.

In an editorial in *Christianity Today* of June 18, 1982, titled "Graham in Moscow, What Did He Really Say?" a reader will find the acknowledgment that disapproval of Billy at that time rose to immense proportions—then the remark "Of course the jury is not in."

Included in the editorial are the words: "But we insist

that the record be set straight. By taking Graham's words out of the context in which they were spoken and putting them in an alien context of their own concerns, some news people consciously or even unconsciously falsified many of Graham's statements. They thus wrongly presented him as belying his own convictions."[2]

In the *Christian Century,* June 23-30, 1982, an article, "How the Press Got it Wrong in Moscow," appeared. Its author, Edward E. Plowman, says:

"As a journalist who travelled with Billy Graham on his recent visit to Moscow, I am disturbed by the questionable quality of much of the media coverage of that event. A towering exception is John Burns of the *New York Times.* Overall, his reporting was perceptive and right on target." He continues, "Normally, I'm defensive when people take pot shots at the press, but I feel constrained to set the record straight in this case. Most of the criticism levelled against Graham in the West, as a result of his visit, rests on distorted and inaccurate reporting. I tape-recorded all of Graham's public talks and almost every one of his many, many press interviews with both Soviet and Western reporters (it was the busiest five day press schedule of his entire life). It is revealing to compare what he actually said with what he is reported to have said."[3]

(Many months after the Moscow trip we understood that the mail at the Billy Graham Association headquarters was running five to one in Billy's favor.)

After the public had been cupping its ear to hear Billy for a few years, someone told Ruth he wasn't a great preacher. Ruth said in effect, "Good! That proves it's the Holy Spirit who is taking his poor efforts and putting his words into the hearts of people all over the world and using them to bring thousands to Christ."

Ruth says of the criticism, "Some of it is justified; much

of it isn't." She once said, "Some writers write with nothing but hate—not even facts, and we can do nothing about it." One person, knowing what she'd said, remarked, "They don't have to do anything about it. "'Vengeance is mine, sayeth the Lord. I will repay.'" Ruth once said, "It's the Lord's problem to handle the criticism," and she believes the Bible when it says "Cast thy burden upon the Lord, and he shall sustain thee" (Ps. 55:22).

Ruth meets all of their critics in one place—on her knees—and deals with them there. But at times she needs the hide of an armadillo to handle some of the criticisms. She makes short shrift of venom.

Billy has said that before he went into evangelism, he read the lives of different evangelists and found that so much of their time was used in answering criticism that they hardly had time to preach the gospel. So he decided that he'd let God handle the criticism for him.

However, when it was reported that he had advised young people to see the picture "Jesus Christ, Superstar," he said he knew it was time to break his silence. He vehemently denied it and said that the film bordered on sacrilege and blasphemy.

Billy has said at times that the media has misquoted him. Some of those who love and respect him most hoped that he was misquoted when he made statements that sounded like he'd gone soft on Communism. Apparently, he felt he'd explained his stand satisfactorily both to them and to God. As always, some agreed and some didn't.

In any event, the mind grows numb when it tries to estimate the numbers who have accepted Christ under his ministry as well as contemplating the countless numbers who *will* accept Christ in the future if God allows him to continue his work.

A friendly reporter once mistakenly called Ruth, "Warm, witty, and worldly." A really sincere Christian avoids worldliness like the plague. Another friendly writer spoke of her as being "of the world." Ruth must have winced because Christ himself warned his followers to be "in the world but not of it." Possibly they were using the wrong terminology, such as was the church member who was introducing her minister and his assistant. She said, "Meet my minister and his accomplice." But Ruth sums up what is said about them by saying, "I don't feel as close to God when things are going too well."

There have been the devoted fans as well as the critics. To the great majority of his fans, it's like firing on the American flag to say a word of criticism of Billy, and they're ready to meet his critics with a hail of lead (pencil). Billy has been a perennial on the list of the most admired men in the United States.

Early on the list, Billy was chosen to appear in the popular program, "The World of. . . ." He was also among the first in the famed Person-to-Person series.

Companies have offered him astonishingly large amounts of money to use his name in connection with their advertising. His father-in-law used to say that Billy had the jitters until he was sure they understood that he wanted no part of their offers.

When he accepted the position of Grand Marshal of the Rose Bowl Parade, he was criticized. He answered that the signs and placards carried by the crowds attending made him feel he was in a revival meeting. Miss U.S.A. of 1981 called Billy "The greatest person living today."

Ethel Waters, the wonderful black woman who thrilled the world with her voice, was once asked if she thought a scheduled crusade of Billy's would be a success. She said, "God don't sponsor no flops."

Billy's hometown, Charlotte, North Carolina, had a Billy Graham Day, honoring Billy. President Nixon was the key speaker. After he spoke, he descended the steps to the tune, "Hail to the Chief," and an unscheduled event took place. Billy's grandson, a little past three, broke loose from his parents, ducked under the velvet ropes, and planted himself squarely in front of the President. He said, with all the confidence of a four-star general, "Hi, Nixon!" Ruth, commenting on it, said, "He should be taken to a taxidermist."

After the celebration, Ruth and Billy received a letter from a fan which said she was really happy that Billy's hometown had seen fit to honor him, but that she wished the little town of Nazareth in Galilee had seen fit to honor the boy who grew up there.

One woman who called herself "Typhoid Mary" said she was a devoted fan of Billy's and that she was always sending him suggestions (which he'd probably already considered and discarded as unworkable). But he'd take the time to send her a note of thanks. Realizing that this was taking valuable time from important duties, she asked him not to answer. On receiving another thank-you note from him, she told him that if he sent any more of them, she'd put his signature up for sale. That ended it, she said.

Politicians running for governor of North Carolina sometimes have come with a photographer to the church that Billy attends at home, in order to be pictured worshiping with him. During a lull in one picture-taking session, Billy spotted a senior citizen who was a friend of the family and went over to give her a peck on the cheek.

Afterward she said despondently, "I tried to hang onto him until the photographer saw us, but no such luck."

Ruth rarely ever gives away the fact that she's Mrs. Billy Graham, but one night in Europe a young woman came into the counseling room after the service. She was overwhelmed by Billy, his message, and the massive response to it. She said to the counselor, who turned out to be Ruth, "I wonder what it would be like to wake up and find yourself married to such a man." Ruth told her that she'd come to the right person to find out. She said, "I've been doing it for eleven years." Later, Ruth said, "I just told her about Jesus."

Ruth is Billy's greatest fan. One magazine, after referring to Billy's five months of amazingly successful crusades in Europe, also mentioned the fact that when he reached his home in North Carolina his doctors told him that he had a kidney stone. Then the writer suggested that surgeons would soon be collecting them.

After the operation, when an overly enthusiastic reporter got Billy to pose with the offending stone, Ruth, in opening up the newspaper and seeing the picture and knowing how hard it was for Billy to say no and not to be gracious, groaned and said, "He needs me to protect him."

Even when Billy's at home, his fans are after him. When Bunny, the youngest daughter, was in the third grade, she invited her daddy to speak to her class during the Easter season. After Bunny had introduced him with much poise and understandable unabashed pride, Billy had his diminutive audience in the palm of his hand when he acknowledged Bunny's introduction by saying, "I think it's very appropriate at the Easter season to have been introduced by a Bunny." He then told his rapt listeners about the real meaning of Easter—the bodily resurrection of Christ.

Ruth and a friend were seated at the kitchen table waiting to hear an address by Billy to be broadcast by radio from Grandfather Mountain. It had been reported that the crowds were so great that cars were backed up bumper to bumper from Grandfather Mountain to Marion, North Carolina. In a little while Billy's voice came over the radio, "Ruth, it looks like I'm going to be late for supper."

The chief of police in Montreat (now city administrator) said, "The greatest honor God has ever given me is the privilege of guarding Billy."

A secretary spoke of the many years she'd worked for Billy and said, "I have yet to see the first inconsistent thing in his life."

Some time ago, I met a lady in a shop where her car was being repaired. She said of Billy, "I feel he is the closest to God of any person on earth." And so it goes. One person remarked about Billy, "When the Lord lays his hand on someone, I take mine off."

Notes

1. From *It's My Turn* by Ruth Bell Graham copyright © 1982 by Ruth Bell Graham. Published by Fleming H. Revell Company. Used by permission.
2. Used by permission.
3. Copyright 1982 Christian Century Foundation. Reprinted by permission from the June 23-30, 1982 issue of *The Christian Century*.

18
All This and Heaven Too

As would be expected, there's a family altar rather than a family bar in the Graham home. Billy and Ruth would agree that it's better to bend the knee rather than the elbow with their children and grandchildren.

Someone has said that drinking is the worst sin because it makes you do all the rest. Some of Billy's and Ruth's aversion to alcohol must have rubbed off on little Franklin because Ruth's secretary was walking down the hall and she heard him in his bedroom shouting with old-time gospel fervor. She cracked the door enough to see him standing on a chair, preaching to his smaller cousin, who was all ears. Franklin had taken his text on the evils of drink and was expounding vehemently, "Drink whiskeeeee and go to hell. Drink orange juice, believe in Jesus, and go to heaven!"

Some of Franklin's "sermon" will be recognized as an echo of Billy's concerns about drinking through the years (Prov. 23:29-35; 1 Cor. 6:10; Prov. 20:1).

The family altar is considered by both Ruth and Billy to be the most important equipment in the home, even though it might not be a literal piece of furniture. Billy says, "I have so many problems and I pray all the time," which is in accord with Paul's words to "Pray without ceasing" (1 Thess. 5:17).

The parents of both Billy and Ruth were indefatigable prayer warriors. Ruth says she can't remember ever getting up in the morning that her dad wasn't reading his Bible, or going to bed at night that he wasn't on his knees praying.

On a memorable day in 1934, a group of Christian businessmen were deeply concerned over world conditions and met in Billy's father's pasture behind the barn to fast and pray. In the group was Vernon Patterson, who remembers that he prayed that "out of Charlotte the Lord would raise up someone to preach the gospel to the ends of the earth." Billy's father later said, "I didn't know I had him on my own place."

Billy remembers that day. When he came home from school and went to the barn to milk the cows, the black helper, who was greatly admired by Billy, told him what was going on in the back lot. Billy threw up his hands and said, "A bunch of religious fanatics!" adding this comment to his already ingrained thinking that his mother's devotions were hogwash. He was later converted under the hellfire and brimstone messages of Mordecai Ham, a fiery revivalist who held a revival in Charlotte.

Who among us is knowledgeable enough to write off a Mordecai Ham or to ring down the curtain on a young Billy Graham who scoffs at Christians, calling them "religious fanatics"? History is replete with accounts of the unlikely ones (like Paul) who have experienced unusual manifestations of the Holy Spirit hovering over, enfolding, and indwelling them.

To Billy, praying is as necessary as breathing. He's often said that he's powerless to accomplish anything without God, who uses Billy's prayers and the prayers of the faithful ones who hold him and his work up before the throne of God. For years there was a woman who went before every crusade to the city where it was to be held. She would rent a room and before and during the crusade, she earnestly prayed for the saving of souls.

Billy has also depended mightily on the prayers of the Holy Spirit who "maketh intercession for us with groanings which cannot be uttered" (Rom. 8:26).

On one occasion when Billy was ill in Hawaii, one of his young daughters was tearfully concerned about his recovery, so she and an older friend joined in prayer for him. Then young Anne recalled, "Sometimes when Daddy comes to the breakfast table, he's too tired to eat." The friend asked, "Why? Hasn't he been resting all night?" Anne said, "One morning he told me he'd been up all night praying." There have been hours on end that Billy has spent prostrate before God in prayer, sometimes known to others, but many times known only to him and God.

In earlier days, Billy went at a furious pace trying to fill every invitation to speak that came down the road, and now and then he went to a masseur to help in unwinding. The masseur, being a new convert, was a little upset because Billy's knees didn't have callouses on them from praying. Billy explained that sometimes Jesus prayed on his knees and sometimes standing and looking up into heaven.

Billy was in the forefront of those starting the movement to get prayer back into the schools; he feels, as do millions of others, that the acceleration of crime and

humanism in the schools is directly related to the re-
moval of prayer and God from the classroom. (William
Murray, on whose behalf prayer was taken out of the
schools, is now a Christian and has gone all out to do
what he can to get it back into the schools.)

Christian Century polled religious editors around the
nation as to the most influential religious leaders in the
United States, and Billy was voted the top spot. His latest
honor is the prestigious Templeton Foundation prize
($200,000) honoring Billy as the Christian who has
preached to more people than anyone who has ever
lived—with over two million (people) accepting Christ
under his ministry. (This doesn't include the many who
have come to Christ, yet haven't registered their commitment.) This award is the religious equivalent of the Nobel
Prize. It was presented by Prince Philip.

Because of his position, hundreds of thousands are
counting on Billy to continue to speak words of hope to a
terrified and hopeless world—the same words he used in
his inaugural prayer when Nixon became president. "If
my people, which are called by my name, shall humble
themselves, and pray, and seek my face, and turn from
their wicked ways; then will I hear from heaven, and will
forgive their sin, and will heal their land" (2 Chron. 7:14).

These words are from the mouth of God himself; they
are spoken to believers, not unbelievers. In a vast gathering recently, Billy gave the example of the wicked city,
Nineveh, which was doomed to certain destruction by the
hand of God. But when their sins were laid on the table
by Jonah, the residents bowed themselves before God in
sincere repentance and begged for his mercy—which he
freely gave as he always has and always will, if we, like
the sinner Jesus told about, will sincerely say, "God be
merciful to me a sinner" (Luke 18:10-14).

When Billy was told that his beliefs were old-fashioned, he said, "Yes, they go back two thousand years to the time of Christ."

Billy has forever made famous the words, "The Bible says." He is the messenger, but the message is God's. With Paul he would say that we preach not ourselves but Christ crucified and risen from the dead. During an era when many ministers have watered down God's Word with human speculation, Billy boldly proclaims what the Bible says God has done, is doing, and will do. Billy would agree with the man who, when questioned as to his acceptance of the miracle of God's having rolled back the waters of the Red Sea to let the Israelites pass over, said, "The thing that bothers me is that anyone could make the Red Sea in the first place. Anybody who could make it could certainly roll it back."

Billy refuses to ad-lib when it comes to the Word of God. He's often said that he's only God's messenger boy— that his job is to deliver God's message without changing it in any way. "Ye shall not add unto the word which I command you, neither shall ye diminish aught from it" (Deut. 4:2).

Ruth has no ho-hum attitude toward the Bible. She says with enthusiasm and flat finality, "I believe every word of it." She's a formidable Bible student; she literally ransacks the Scriptures. The desk in her room often has several translations open on it, and anyone tangling with her as to Scriptures had better know what he's talking about or he'll soon find himself out over his depth. Julie Eisenhower wrote about Ruth that Ruth's Bible is so old and used that it rolls like a magazine. She also mentioned the fact that a belt wrapped around it holds and protects it.

Though both Billy and Ruth are avid readers of the

many books that line the shelves in their home and Billy's office, I think I'm safe in saying that to both of them, there's really only one book—the Bible.

Noah Webster said, "Education is useless without the Bible." Sir Isaac Newton said, "If all the great books of the world were given life and brought together in convention, the moment the Bible entered, the other books would fall on their faces."

Billy puts so much emphasis on Scripture because Scripture itself does, declaring, "All scripture is given by inspiration of God" (2 Tim. 3:16) and "Holy men of God spake as they were moved by the Holy Ghost" (2 Pet. 1:21). Christ *is* the living Word. Scripture is the written word bearing witness to the living Word.

Billy considers it the final word when Christ himself speaks about Scripture. The following are some of Christ's profound words regarding the Bible: "Search the scriptures; for in them ye think ye have eternal life: and they are they which testify of me" (John 5:39).

"Ye . . . err, because ye know not the scriptures, neither the power of God" (Mark 12:24).

"The scripture cannot be broken" (John 10:35).

"He that rejecteth me, and receiveth not my words, hath one that judgeth him: the word that I have spoken, the same shall judge him in the last day" (John 12:48).

"He that is of God heareth God's words; ye therefore hear them not because ye are not of God" (John 8:47).

"O fools, and slow of heart to believe all that the prophets have spoken" (Luke 24:25).

"Heaven and earth shall pass away, but my words shall not pass away" (Matt. 24:35).

"For verily I say unto you, Till heaven and earth pass, one jot or one tittle shall in no wise pass from the law, till all be fulfilled" (Matt. 5:18). (The dotting of an "i" or the crossing of a "t.")

"For had ye believed Moses, ye would have believed me: for he wrote of me. But if ye believe not his writings, how shall ye believe my words?" (John 5:46-47).

"Man shall not live by bread alone but by every word that proceedeth out of the mouth of God" (Matt. 4:4).

"Verily, verily, I say unto you, He that heareth my word, and believeth on him that sent me, hath everlasting life, and shall not come into condemnation (judgment); but is passed from death unto life" (John 5:24).

"Well hath Esaias prophesied of you hypocrites, as it is written, This people honoureth me with their lips, but their heart is far from me. Howbeit in vain do they worship me, teaching for doctrines the commandments of men. For laying aside the commandment of God, ye hold the tradition of men. . . . Full well ye reject the commandment of God, that ye may keep your own tradition" (Mark 7:6-9).

Jesus often said, "It is written," quoting Scripture. Recalling Scripture, he'd say, "Have you not read—?" During his temptation by Satan, he routed him by quoting Scripture.

From Christ's own words, it would seem that anyone who fails to hear (accept) God's word is left holding the bag—a religious rag bag. To Christ, the Bible isn't a spiritual snack tray from which a person can take off some things and leave others. He even calls a person a fool who doesn't believe *all* that the prophets have spoken. Billy believes *all* of it. The Old Testament was the only Scripture that Christ had.

Nation after nation has been fired up by Billy's flaming messages as he says to all who will listen, "God is love," but also "God is just," and for those who reject his proffered love, there awaits eternal punishment.

However, he stresses the biblical truth that hell is optional because God, in his incredible love, has provided a sure way of escape from hell through the death and resurrection of his only Son, who went to the cross to pay in full for our sin and guilt—taking on himself our sins and giving us in return his perfect righteousness ("swapping" with us, as someone has put it). By accepting this free gift and repenting of our sins, we are in turn accepted as children of God and joint heirs with Jesus Christ, with the full assurance that nothing can pluck us out of his hand as we look forward to a glorious eternity in his presence.

But not everyone believes in hell, though Jesus himself said more about hell than he did heaven, and his words about hell are the most vivid in the Bible (Luke 16:20-31; Matt. 25:30-41; Mark 9:43-49).

Billy has always felt it was inconsistent for anyone to accept Christ's words about heaven yet reject his words about hell. But the idea of hell is often belittled; and more often than not, Satan is portrayed as a comical figure in a jaunty red jumpsuit with horns and a tail.

When Billy was asked, "You don't think a loving God would allow a person to go to hell, do you?" Billy answered, "Yes, but not willingly." Whether a person accepts or rejects Christ's words, Billy continues to preach the words of the Bible, "It is a fearful thing to fall into the hands of the living God" (Heb. 10:31). Some seem to look on God as a sort of Jolly Green Giant, but the picture in Proverbs 1:24-33 is entirely different. However, in this age of grace, we still have the promise, "Let the wicked forsake his way, and the unrighteous man his thoughts: and let him return unto the Lord, and . . . he will abundantly pardon" (Isa. 55:7). This is the glorious message that has been trumpeted from every lectern behind which Billy has spoken from the time he first accepted the call to evangelize.

For many years numerous books, magazines, and newspapers have printed the dying words of certain famous unbelievers as they themselves admittedly faced an eternal hell. The most recent account I read included the names of Sir Walter Scott, Sir Francis Newport, Volney, Mirabeau, and Voltaire. Their words and actions are too horrifying to record here. Suffice it to give the words of Voltaire's nurse: "For all the wealth of Europe, I would not watch another infidel die."

In a day when the preaching of the cross and the blood is to many a "slaughterhouse religion," Billy continues to preach the words of the Bible. "Without shedding of blood is no remission" (Heb. 9:22). "The blood of Jesus his Son cleanseth us from all sin" (1 John 1:7). "For the preaching of the cross is to them that perish foolishness; but unto us which are saved it is the power of God" (1 Cor. 1:18).

Billy preaches that Christ is the one and only way to God. He preaches as does the Bible that a person's salvation depends solely on Christ plus nothing and no one. An immense banner at one of his Crusades proclaimed, "I am the way, the truth and the life. No man cometh to the father but by me" (John 14:6). Jesus says that he is the door; and that anyone climbing up any other way is a thief and a robber (John 10:1). Also see the verse, "Neither is there salvation in any other; for there is none other name under heaven given among men, whereby we must be saved" (Acts 4:12). (Billy knows that this isn't a popular message in a day when syncretism is preached from many pulpits.)

Billy preaches that it is through the grace of Christ (unmerited favor) that a person is saved, apart from good works. "For by grace are ye saved through faith; and that not of yourselves: it is the gift of God: Not of works, lest any man should boast" (Eph. 2:8-9). "But if by grace, then is it no more of works; otherwise grace is no more grace" (Rom. 11:6). "Not by works of righteousness . . . we have done, but according to his mercy he saved us" (Titus 3:5). (Christians perform good works *because* they're saved—not in order to *be* saved.)

Billy preaches the words of the Bible that everyone but Christ himself has sinned and needs a Savior. "For all have sinned and come short of the glory of God" (Rom. 3:23). "There is none that doeth good, no, not one" (Rom. 3:12). See Mary's words in Luke 1:47, "My spirit hath rejoiced in God, my Savior."

Billy preaches that if a person repents of his sin and accepts Christ as Lord and Savior, he is forgiven: "If we confess our sins, he is faithful and just to forgive us our sins and to cleanse us from all unrighteousness" (1 John 1:9). "There is therefore now no condemnation to them which are in Christ Jesus, who walk not after the flesh, but after the Spirit" (Rom. 8:1).

In many places in Scripture, Christians are told how Christ deals with their sins: They are cast into the depths of the sea (Mic. 7:19), blotted out as a thick cloud (Isa. 44:22), cast behind God's back (Isa. 38:17), made as white as snow (Isa. 1:18), removed as far as the east is from the west (Ps. 103:12). Note also that Christians can have the certain knowledge that they're saved. "These things have I written unto you that believe on the name of the Son of God; that ye may *know that ye have eternal life*" (italics added, 1 John 5:13).

Billy recalls Christ's triumphant words from the cross, "It is finished," and takes them to mean exactly what they say. He preaches from Heb. 9:25-26: "Nor yet that he should offer himself often . . . For then must he often have suffered since the foundation of the world: but now once in the end of the world hath he appeared to put away sin by the sacrifice of himself." "But this man, after he had offered one sacrifice for sins for ever, sat down on the right hand of God" (Heb. 10:12).

"Knowing that Christ being raised from the dead dieth no more; death hath no more dominion over him" (Rom. 6:9).

In spite of the fact that some preach and teach that everyone will be saved, Billy sticks to Christ's own words that only a few will find eternal life (Matt. 7:13-14). Since it's their word against Christ's, Billy relies wholly on the words of Christ. (Moody Adams fairly recently quoted Billy as saying that 85 to 95 percent of those on church rolls were not born again.) Jesus says, "Ye must be born again" (John 3:7).

Billy preaches that by Christ's one and only sacrifice, a believer is made perfect forever. "We are sanctified through the offering of the body of Jesus Christ once for all" (Heb. 10:10).

He preaches from Luke 5:20-26 that only God can forgive sins. He preaches from God's Word that salvation is free. "The wages of sin is death; but the gift of God is eternal life through Jesus Christ our Lord" (Rom. 6:23). "They that trust in their wealth and boast themselves in the multitude of their riches; none of them can by any means redeem his brother, nor give to God a ransom for him: (for the redemption of their soul is precious, and it ceaseth for ever)" (Ps. 49:6-8). "Thy money perish with thee, because thou hast thought that the gift of God could be purchased with money" (Acts 8:20).

Billy preaches the second coming of Christ. He said that if anyone had asked him some years ago if he thought the Lord's return might be soon, he'd have said, "I don't know." He continues, "I don't say that anymore." Usually his last televised sermon after holding a crusade is on the subject of the return of Christ. The Graham Christmas card for 1981 referred to Jesus' coming. Billy recently mentioned the twenty-fifth chapter of Matthew as a place where his listeners could find information about Christ's return. He has given Luke 21:7-36 as Christ's own predictions of the last days and Mark 13:1-37 as referring to happenings that will precede his return. For those who scoff, Billy has pointed out that they are fulfilling the prophecy of 2 Peter 3:3.

According to the *New York Times,* one of the best-selling books of the past ten years has the second coming of Christ at the heart of its content. The book is *The Late Great Planet Earth* by Hal Lindsey (Grand Rapids: Zondervan, 1974). Evidently many people are interested in reading about the end of this age and the return of Christ.

The Bible suggests a "prime time" appearance when Christ returns—"Every eye shall see him" (Rev. 1:7). Consequently, considering all of the other signs given, many Bible students preaching and writing on the subject have inspired a sky watch in countless places all over the world as television, radio, and reading audiences are being alerted and saturated as never before in history to the possibility and probability of the Lord's return soon. In one interview with Billy the subject came up about people who were looking for Christ's return soon, and Billy answered, "They're probably right."

All of the children, as well as Billy and Ruth, feel that the biblical signs are now in place and that Christ could come at any time. But aside from that, thoughts of worldwide destruction have never before in history been more on people's minds. Millions feel that all of us are on Death Row, not knowing when the time of our exit shall come. But Billy preaches that for the Christian there should be no terror because the Bible says, "Absent from the body, . . . present with the Lord" (2 Cor. 5:8).

With all of these things on her mind, one day Ruth was speaking of her imperfections to a group of women and telling them how God was guiding and correcting her. Then she recalled two road signs she'd seen on the way to the meeting. The first one said, "Road Under Construction." There were many bumps, holes, and rough spots before she finally came to the sign, "End of Construction. Thank You for Your Patience." Ruth added, "I'd like to have that on my tombstone."

As for Billy, as you sit in the living room of this home and watch as the flames in the cavernous fireplace dapple the room with shadows, the thought intrudes that even as you consider the mundane details in the home, you must of necessity recognize the fact that the head of this house has been singularly touched by God.

You feel the awe and mystery of the mountain stillness—and somehow the feeling persists (even though you know it's unfounded) that you're on at least a small patch of holy ground. And for a fleeting moment, a sort of cathedral hush envelops you.

You're perfectly aware of the fact that the man sitting across the room from you is a man like other men, with admittedly many human frailties. Yet somehow he is vastly different—unique in the history of the world—and proof that God keeps his treasure in earthen vessels as his Word declares.

Suddenly, as if tortured by the small talk in the room and as though tuned in to a voice not heard by the others, he bounds from his chair. Your eyes follow as the tall, disciplined, rangy figure goes through the door and into the yard which has been called "a platform between earth and heaven." An eerie, deepening twilight dusts the scene. He sits on the locust fence far above the little mountain town—and you wonder that his mind doesn't burst with the almost superhuman pressures.

As you ponder the whys and wherefores of this man's life, you recall an incident in the life of the late King George. One day he visited a china factory. He picked up a vase which had not yet been fired—and left in the soft clay the print of his hand. He felt that he had ruined the vase, but the factory owner knew better. Because of the print of the king's hand on it, the vase had become infinitely more valuable. Because of the clear and unmistakable print of the hand of the King of Kings on Billy's life, it too has become infinitely more valuable.

As you continue to ponder, you offer up a prayer that God will keep his hand on Billy until that day when he's on his way to claim the promise of God that "They that be wise shall shine as the brightness of the firmament; and they that turn many to righteousness as the stars for ever and ever" (Dan. 12:3).